October/November
2011

— Happy Un-birthday!

Love, NAN

THE ARCHITECTURAL HERITAGE OF THE PISCATAQUA

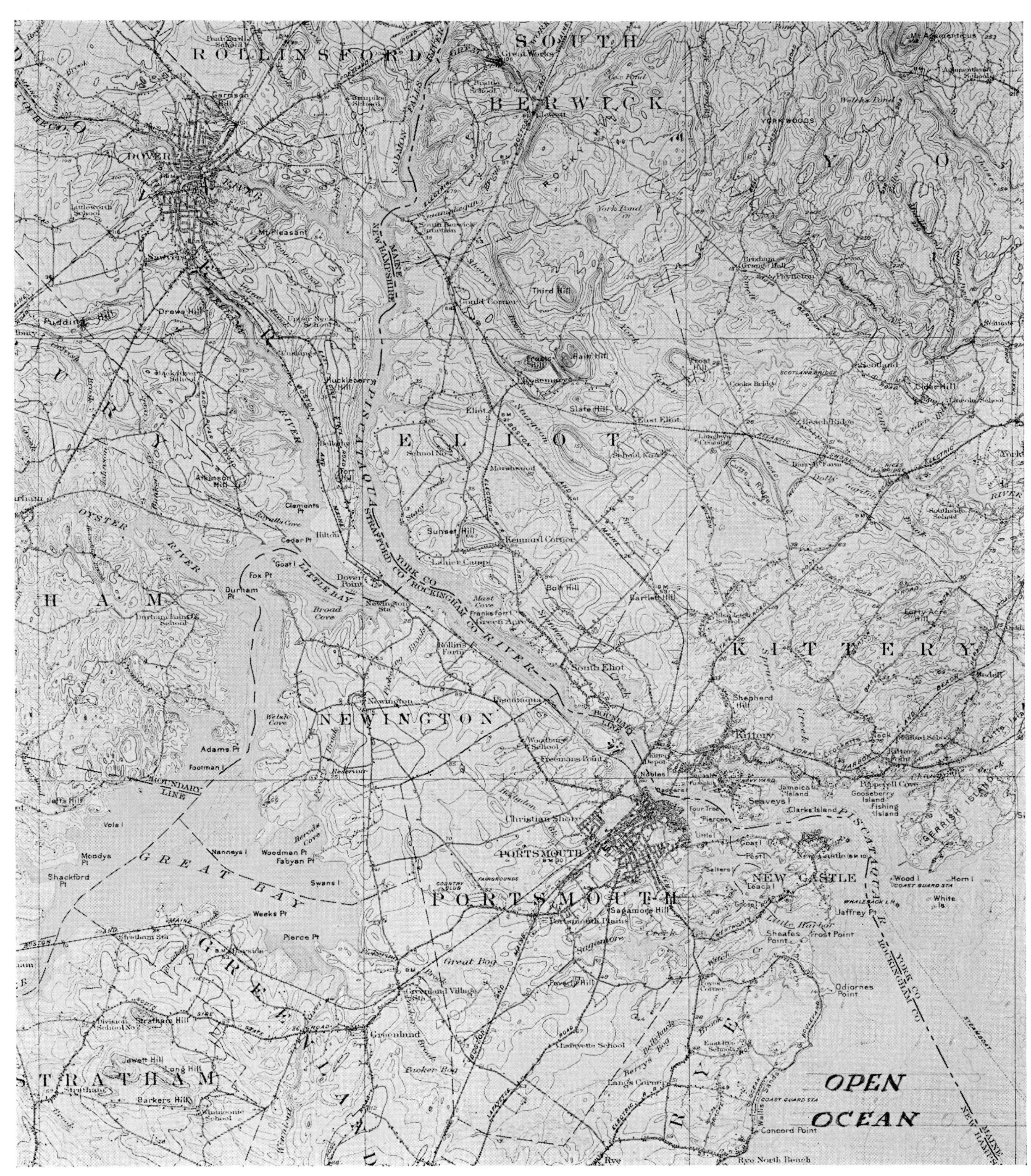

Portsmouth District and the Piscataqua River which forms the boundary line between Maine and New Hampshire.

A PISCATAQUA PRODUCT

From the

U. S. Steam Frigate Lancaster

Built at Philadelphia Navy Yard, 1858

Length 235 Ft. Beam 46 Ft. Tonnage 3250

Eagle carved when the vessel was reconditioned in 1880 at the Portsmouth Navy Yard on the Piscataqua
by John Haley Bellamy
Celebrated Wood Carver of Kittery Point, Maine.

The above is from the label attached to this remarkable exhibit in the MARINERS' MUSEUM at Newport News, Virginia.

John Bellamy was born at Kittery Point, Maine, in 1836 in the old Mansion house of Sir William Pepperrell from whom he was descended. His father was one of the commissioners to Great Britain whose work resulted in the Ashburton Treaty. Bellamy studied art in Boston and New York but finally became a carver of figureheads, etc.

This eagle stands ten feet high and, could it spread its wings, would have a wing-spread of 30 feet or more.

THE ARCHITECTURAL HERITAGE OF THE PISCATAQUA

HOUSES AND GARDENS OF THE PORTSMOUTH DISTRICT OF MAINE AND NEW HAMPSHIRE

BY

JOHN MEAD HOWELLS

with an introduction by

WILLIAM LAWRENCE BOTTOMLEY

and foreword by

RICHARD HUBBARD HOWLAND

WHALESBACK BOOKS

WASHINGTON, D.C.

Publisher's Note: This book was first published in 1937 by The Architectural Book Publishing Co. and was re-printed in 1966, '69, '72 and '78 by Outlet Book Co. The present publisher wishes to acknowledge the permission of The Architectural Book Publishing Co. to use the original negatives to re-publish this book. This edition includes a new foreward by Richard Hubbard Howland, former President of The National Trust for Historic Preservation.

1988 WHALESBACK BOOKS, Box 9546 Washington, D.C. 20016
Printed on acid-free paper and bound by Arcata Graphics, Kingsport, TN

Library of Congress Cataloging-in-Publication Data.

Howells, John Mead, 1868 - 1959
The architectural heritage of the Piscataqua.

Reprint. Originally published: New York : Architectural Book Pub. Co., c1937.
"Books on architecture and the allied crafts used in America prior to 1830": p.
Includes index.
1. Architecture, Colonial—Piscataqua River Valley (N.H. and Me.) 2. Historic buildings—Piscataqua River (N.H. and Me.) I. Title.
NA715.H69 1988 728.3' 7' 097426 88-20768
ISBN 0-929590-00-7 (alk. paper)

FOREWORD

This fifth reprinting of John Mead Howells' survey of America's early architectural treasures, in recognition of the fiftieth anniversary of its original appearance, testifies to its enduring value as an historic documentary, as an architectural reference and as an impetus for historic preservation. Its re-appearance coincides with a renewed interest in the work of William Lawrence Bottomley, whose scholarly Introduction below remains a gem of architectural literature, and, more importantly, with the maturation of Portsmouth's restoration effort under Strawbery Banke, Inc. which has fulfilled John Mead Howells' inspiration for the preservation of the architectural heritage of Portsmouth and the Piscataqua region envisioned in this book.

Bottomley's extensive architectural practice is now receiving deserved critical attention and he is currently referred to as one of the finest American architects of the first half of the twentieth century, arguably our most skilled traditional residential designer after 1925. His work was mostly in the Georgian tradition, but his River House in New York City, built in 1932 on the shore of the East River, still stands as America's most significant Art Deco apartment house. His designs for important residences in Virginia, in the Tidewater style, are reminiscent of the "Banker's Georgian" mansions of Sir Edward Lutyens in England.

The bibliography on architecture and allied crafts used in America prior to 1830 that Bottomley included in his Introduction to this volume is a first-rate, scholarly compendium that is very useful indeed today. His essay on the design and construction of early houses, with informative plans and diagrams, is also timeless and might well be reprinted as a separate mongraph beneficial to both professionals and laymen.

Bottomley, a friend of Howells, was born in New York in 1883 of a distinguished Irish family (his maternal uncle was Lord Kelvin who invented the process which led to the Kelvinator refrigerator.) In the same year that he wrote the Introduction to this book, he edited Volumes I and II of *Great Georgian Houses of America* from which were drawn several illustrations and measured drawings of Portsmouth houses appearing here. These two volumes of Bottomley's together with this one by Howells published in 1937-38 were important milestones on the path of the preservation movement in America that had already received a tremendous impetus from the inauguration of Williamsburg's restoration programs in the preceding two years. Some twenty years later, the future of at least part of Portsmouth's architectural heritage which both Howells and Bottomley so admired was secured by the incorporation on November 19, 1958, of Strawbery Banke, Inc. This unique and splendid organization was the result in part of the influence of this book. It owes its origins, which I was fortunate to witness, to the remarkable efforts and hard work of a small group which included Howells' daughter-in-law, Muriel Seabury Howells, Dr. Dorothy Vaughan, Librarian of the Portsmouth Library who had aided Howells in the research for this book, Andrew H. Jarvis, then Mayor of Portsmouth, and several others who understood the importance of Portsmouth's architectural preservation.

The Strawbery Banke project, named for the original settlement that later became Portsmouth, centers around a neighborhood that once rimmed a small, shallow inlet called Puddle Dock. Here the new organization restored several small houses that were on the site and assumed stewardship of several that were moved in from other parts of the city. Much of this undertaking was associated with an enlightened urban renewal project in which public funds were used to clear slums, rehabilitate the Puddle Dock area, and save a number of buildings that would otherwise have fallen to the wrecker's ball. Now, after thirty years, Strawbery Banke, Inc. is well established and flourishing; five of the historic properties featured in this book have come into its caring hands to be protected forever along with several dozen other structures in the historic area dating from the 17th to early 20th centuries.

The reader's attention is invited to the photograph shown as Figure 116 of the Captain Samuel Chauncey House which once graced Islington Street but was demolished in 1936 to make way for a filling station. This picture helped to galvanize public support nationwide for the preservation movement in the 1950's; together with a photograph of the succeeding gas station, it was used as a before-and-after presentation in scores of lectures and symposia organized by the National Trust for Historic Preservation throughout the country to dramatize the urgent need for preservation of America's architectural heritage. This picture not only helped arouse the interest of a very wide audience but led directly to the intervention and aid on the part of the National Trust's staff to help in the establishment of Strawbery Banke, Inc. and its adjunct supporting organization, The Guild of Strawbery Banke. I am proud and pleased to have been part of this effort.

RICHARD HUBBARD HOWLAND
July, 1988

CHRONOLOGY

NOTES ON EARLY VISITS TO, AND SETTLEMENTS IN THE PISCATAQUA REGION
COMPILED FOR THE GARDEN CLUB OF AMERICA IN 1934.

There seem to have been a great number of visits to the shores of this part of New England by adventurers in search of the North West Passage, of good fishing grounds, or of the leaves of the sassafras, for which there was a great demand in the seventeenth century. But those who left a record are, first, Capt. Bartholomew Gosnold in 1602, and then, in 1603, Martin Pring, with two ships and a company of forty-three men. He described the Kennebec, Saco, York and Piscataqua Rivers, and found plenty of fish, but none of the precious sassafras. George Weymouth made the voyage in 1605 and took captive, to England, five Indians. In 1606 Sir John Popham sent an expedition which lingered for a year at the mouth of the Kennebec. In 1614 no less a person than Capt. John Smith paid a visit to the Isles of Shoals (which he named "Smith's Islands") and drew a map of the coast, which he showed to King Charles. Charles named the country "New England." Captain Smith was an intimate friend of Sir Ferdinando Gorges and it is possible that his descriptions influenced Sir Ferdinando, and Capt. John Mason, in 1622, to ask for a grant of land, from the Merrimac to the Kennebec, as their share of the new world.

The first permanent settler in the vicinity was David Thompson who arrived in 1623 with his wife, and with ten other men. He built a house at "Pannaway", now Odiorne's Point, New Hampshire. There seems to be some confusion as to whether Thompson came as an agent of Mason and Gorges, or with a conflicting patent of his own. At any rate, when Captain Mason's ship appeared in 1630, Thompson left his plantation and settled on his island in Boston Harbor, still known as "Thompson's Island." Mason, who held the post of Governor of Newfoundland for six years, never saw his demesne here, and although he supplied it with money, provisions and cattle, as well as with colonists, it is doubtful if he received in return as much as he spent on it. He had divided the grant with Gorges, taking for his share the westerly half, from the Merrimac up to, and including, Berwick. He died in 1635 and his stewards in this country appropriated his possessions and chose one of themselves to be "Governor of the Pascataway Plantations"; the future state of New Hampshire.

Sir Ferdinando Gorges held the Province of Maine, extending from the Piscataqua to the Kennebec River, and he founded the first city in America—"Gorgeana," the present town of York. He, like Mason, never visited the land of which he was Lord Proprietor. In 1677 the Commonwealth of Massachusetts purchased the tract from his grandson for 1250 pounds, and it remained part of Massachusetts until it became a state in 1820. The history of Maine for 143 years is the history of Massachusetts, but very distinctive for all that. The early settlers sent out by Gorges were industrious and courageous, but they did not come for reasons of religion. They came for trade; and the coast of Maine was busy and prosperous. The savage Abenakis were held in check, while dignified and beautiful dwellings were being built, and ships were being constructed in the sheltered bays. There were four magnificent Pepperrell mansions at Kittery Point. Three still exist, including the earliest (1689) where Sir William was born. At York and South Berwick the sawmills were used not only to prepare wood for shipment to England, but also to produce the big pine boards for panelling the owner's Drawing Rooms. At York, also, in 1761, the first pile draw-bridge in America was designed and built by Major Samuel Sewell. And at Badgers Island, Kittery, at the entrance to the future State of Maine, the frigate Ranger was built for Capt. John Paul Jones, to fight the British. The present bridge across the Piscataqua is a memorial to the men who fought side by side with the British in the World War.

A. W. H.

MEMORANDA ON AN EARLY PORTSMOUTH BUILDER AND OF POSSIBLE ARCHITECTS AND SOURCES OF DESIGN

C. W. Brewster, writing in 1853 speaks of a then "aged man" telling him that he well remembered the building of the houses of John K. Pickering, and of Col. Oliver Whipple, both of which must have been of a good type.

Said this aged man, "All the houses were alike, of two stories with gambrel roofs and were built by Hopestil March of Dover, a Mulatto—But O! what a change there has been since the Revolution."

Again "in 1743 Paul March built the Bell Tavern as owner. The building was framed by Hopestill Caswell, a Mulatto, a half brother of Paul March."

This mulatto being illegitimate, may have been variously called and was probably the same man. But what interests us is that these notes show that at least an average house of the time was built and probably laid out or designed by a clever mulatto carpenter and apparently without drawings, and much less an architect.

As to design, he probably copied one house from another, varying each by discussions with the next owner and probably copying and varying entrance doors, cornices, porches and even staircases as they went along. Perhaps for decorative doorways, and stairs, and mantels, ships carpenters and carvers or even men like McIntire of Salem were consulted, but all this is conjecture.

It was fashionable for gentlemen to understand architecture and men like Jefferson and others of his class, had books and copperplates of the designs of Sir William Chambers and the Adam Brothers and others. Then by the time of Bulfinch's return from England in 1787 the great cities either had architects in practice or coming temporarily from abroad like Peter Harrison in Boston or Jay in Savannah—but how the New England towns, for instance, developed their designs before the Revolution is not clear, unless such builders also had access to books and plates on design, and even housesmiths like Hopestill Caswell were capable of using them.

As for which, if any, Portsmouth houses were designed by Bulfinch, Gurney says the Public Library originally built for an Academy was "erected in 1806 from designs by Charles Bulfinch, the eminent architect who designed the Massachusetts State House." This building is not mentioned in Bulfinch's own list of his works which was found among his papers after his death. This list however evidently contains only such buildings as Bulfinch considered important. For instance, none of the splendid residences known to be by him are mentioned. The Capitol at Augusta, Maine, is omitted as is also the City Hall at Hartford, Conn. This list therefore is certainly not a complete one. However as the Augusta Capitol was nearly his last work—it is possible that this list was compiled earlier and never completed.

A coincidence of design which might indicate Bulfinch is noted in connection with the Larkin-Rice House on another plate.

The writer has only once before noticed the singular window treatment, which is identical with the Burd House in Philadelphia, long since destroyed, of which a photograph is shown by Fiske Kimball in his invaluable book. That house was by Latrobe, who preceded Bulfinch as architect of the Capitol at Washington. Bulfinch admired Latrobe's work and must have been familiar with the Burd House.

Also the following is interesting to architects. Gurney says "There formerly stood on the South corner of Middle Street and Richards Avenue, one of the finest designed and unique residences in the city bearing the mark of an architect like Bulfinch."

Old photographs show a three story brick house symmetrical on a 45° axis, on a corner, very like the Octagon in Washington which was designed by Dr. Thornton who won the competition for the capitol. They are both clever plans and so much alike that it seems likely that someone who had seen and admired Thornton's work must have designed it. This might well be Bulfinch who followed both Thornton and Latrobe on the Capitol.

There are some resemblances between certain houses in this Piscataqua district that make one think that the same hand designed them. For instance the general type of the Gov. Langdon House together with the cornices, dormer windows, roof-type, etc. will recall at once Hamilton House on the Piscataqua at So. Berwick. The Chinese balustrade of Hamilton House, now gone, was perhaps another point of resemblance. The outer wall of the great drawing rooms in both are identical in treatment inside. The date of one is 1784, the other perhaps 1775. It is interesting to note the carving on the parlor mantel of the Gov. John Wentworth House (1769) and to see how identical it is with the carving over the entrance to the Lady Pepperrell House at Kittery Point (1760).

These are desultory memoranda on features and coincidences noted—and are only valuable as such.

I have limited myself to styles of buildings beginning with the 17th Century types and going on through the Greek Revival so called. Portsmouth seems to have escaped much of the Eastlake type of house, though many fine parlors show their Colonial mantelpieces lost in a wealth of wallpapers, borders and dados of the imitators of William Morris, Walter Crane and even Oscar Wilde. Really good examples, however, of this period are the Hotel Rockingham interiors. Portsmouth never had the prosperity and development that did away with the old Dutch town of New York, or the English Colonial towns of Boston and Philadelphia.

And so it seemed to me interesting to present everything that is left of Portsmouth, not only the Great Houses, but quite as much the large quantity of every day types of the earlier times.

THE AUTHOR

"When a town has a personality of its own, is it not entitled to a biography?"

M. A. DE WOLF HOWE

METHODS OF DESIGN AND CONSTRUCTION OF OUR EARLY DAYS

by William Lawrence Bottomley.

In a young country like ours the growth and development is rapid, and changes in modes of life, methods of business and styles of architecture follow each other with great rapidity. It has been the fate of the best buildings in most of our larger cities to be destroyed prematurely. In Boston, Philadelphia and especially in New York, the growth of new business and residential sections, and the abandonment of old, have completely changed these towns so many times that only a small proportion of the fine early buildings now remain. Fortunately, records are available of almost every type of plan and style of construction that was ever used so that with study one may gain a clear idea of the life and appearance of our early towns in any section of the Atlantic Seaboard. A valuable work was recently published, also by Mr. John Mead Howells, entitled "Lost Examples of Colonial Architecture", which records many fine and varied types of buildings no longer in existence.

A few important towns survive today with much of their early work complete and extant—Charleston, Annapolis and Portsmouth. It is in Portsmouth, however, that the most complete record remains in a good state.

The three hundred photographs and drawings of the architecture and gardens of Portsmouth and its vicinity which compose this volume give a vivid picture of a prosperous American town in the Colonial and Early Federal Periods of our history. The very fact that it is the most complete record so far published of any locality throws a doubly intense light on the origins and methods of work by which our unique and beautiful early style was evolved. Here are presented the public buildings and churches but more particularly examples of types of houses from the first simple ones to the largest and most elaborately designed, houses of large places in the country, and town houses; houses of weather boarding, shingles and brick. The types of plan represent the main types of New England and here also are shown the various kinds of roofs, windows and doors and beautiful examples of interior and exterior detail.

There are several reasons why Portsmouth has remained so intact. Its early days were active although it never was a great center. With a good harbor on the broad and deep Piscataqua River, the development of a wide and fertile surrounding countryside and unlimited fine timber for ship building it soon became an important port. From Colonial days until the early part of the XIX Century the development was steady. Gradually, thereafter, the shipping left it. The trading with the East and with Europe gave way to the development of the country as a career for the most enterprising men at this time. After the war of 1812 manufacturing and the conquest of the land to the West as far as the Valley of the Mississippi gained greater momentum. Boston, New York, Philadelphia and Savannah being on direct main routes to the interior of the country, grew by leaps and bounds. Portsmouth, on the other hand, was not on any great line of communications. It continued comfortably prosperous but was far outstripped by many other cities. The clipper ship trade continued until after the civil war when even that suffered a decline. There was enough wealth and enough trade to keep things up but not enough to require more and larger buildings and thus destroy the old.

A further reason for its lack of growth was the lack of development of manufacturing. Certainly one important reason for that was the presence of the Navy Yard. In the Colonial period manufacturing was carried on in small shops and mostly by individuals. After the Revolution, and at the same time the Navy was being developed, manufacturing became a more and more important factor in the development of our towns. Charleston, Annapolis, Newport and Portsmouth all developed early and with great promise. They each later became the site of a a naval base and yard. In a small town, however, the constant call for men with steady work at a Navy Yard takes a large proportion of the best workers. Manufacturers found that this competition in a limited labor market was disadvantageous and although a number of factories were started, most of them either petered out or moved away.

There thus remains in Portsmouth, what may be described as an Architectural Sequence. In other words, although not on the scale of the large cities, and in spite of the fire of 1813 which wiped out much of the early town, there still remains here an astonishing body or mass of old buildings, especially houses. I describe it as a mass because there are parts of the town where many old buildings stand side by side in their original groups to an extent not to be seen in other places. In the old Maritime quarter around and beyond what was once Puddle Dock there are visible to-day tiny streets, very short, with no sidewalks, like an old English town. If one stands looking down some of these little dead-ends toward the water, as for instance Franklin Street, one's eyes to-day see almost exactly what they would have seen, had one been standing there in cocked hat and shoebuckles in Revolutionary times.

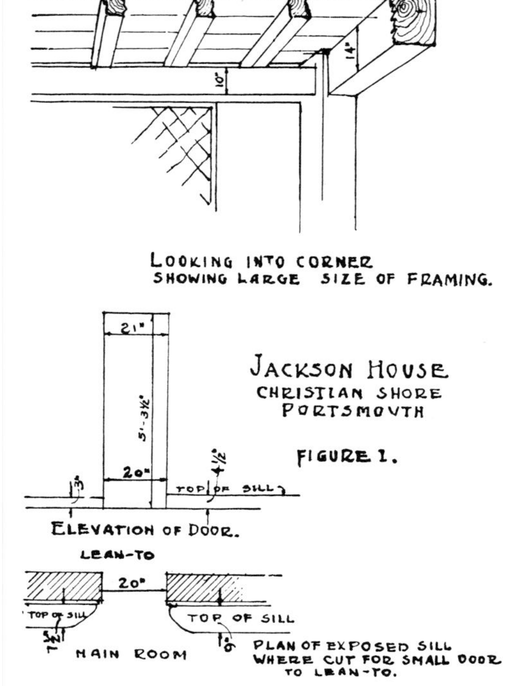

This is precisely what makes Portsmouth unique, it is the mass of houses, great and small, which is so unchanged that it presents a complete sequence. And the Architect or any other lover of old buildings can pick out for himself buildings of any period of activity since the middle of the XVIIth Century.

This can no longer be true in New York, once a beautiful and flourishing Dutch town, nor in Boston, once a picture of a Colonial English City because the body and mass of the little old buildings is gone. In each great city, Philadelphia, Boston or New York—there are fortunately well preserved famous old buildings. Independence Hall, the Boston State House, or the New York City Hall. These isolated examples, however fine do not form a sequence nor give a living picture of the past as does Portsmouth.

Going back to the first buildings put up by the settlers in this Country we find sod roofed dug-outs, a tent like round building built of wattles thatched, sodded or daubed with mud, and one room sheds nearly square with steep roofs. Prototypes of these forms may be found in England and were once more common. They are the quickest and easiest shelters to build and almost all of them have disappeared long ago. In Salem a restoration of several of these types has recently been made. In England, as Fiske Kimball points out in "The Domestic Architecture of the Colonies and the Early Republic", one may see huts built by charcoal burners similar to some described by the early settlers, and as for the sod roof dug-outs and sod walled huts they are frequently seen even to-day.

Among the first arrivals here the building trades were well represented and mention is made in the early records of the Colonies of "massons", "joyners", "sawyers", "naylers", "thatchers", "ryvers of clapboards, shinglers and lathers" and carpenters. Long apprenticeships taught them thoroughly the technique and traditions of their various trades and with their English background coupled with the conservative point of view of the English people it is natural that the first buildings put up followed as closely as possible the buildings with which they were familiar at home within the limits of materials at hand. Cellars were small or non-existent, the stones usually laid in mud or clay but the stones were well fitted and frequently neatly squared. The framing of the superstructure following the tradition of the English half timbered houses was made of oak of great weight and strength, roughly squared with a broad-axe, mortised and tennoned and pinned together with oak dowels. Pine, spruce, hemlock, chestnut, poplar and maple would have been easier to work and could be had in abundance but the English tradition was so strong that the use of oak was practically universal. The solidity of these old buildings attest to-day to the wisdom of this choice. Differing from the small English house the walls, instead of being parged with clay and plaster over wattles or brick and roofed with thatch, at a very early date were given a completely different treatment. Owing to the fiercer storms, heavier winds, torrential "Easters" and "Nor-easters", heavy thunder storms and the greater extremes of heat and cold, the English wall and roof treatments were not practicable or durable. From almost the first, clapboards were used as wall coverings, and shingles or slabs for the roof. Leaded casements at first used, as may be seen in the old Jackson house, (circa 1664), North West Street, in Portsmouth, soon gave way to the newer English style of double-hung wooden sashes glazed with small panes of blown glass.

This Jackson house which is one of the rare early houses in this country has several unusual features, not only are its plan, its great chimney, its gables, and small leaded casement windows characteristic of the houses in England of an earlier age but it well illustrates the methods used by the early builders. Figure I shows the heavy corner posts and girts which are exposed in the rooms. These are heavier than necessary and were laid out by its builders according to tradition rather than any structural necessity of strength. Figure VI shows a rare method of setting the sills. In stead of laying them on top of the foundation walls and framing the floor timbers into them at the top in the usual way after the foundation and floor beams were installed these sills which vary in size up to 9″ x 12″ were laid on top of the floor beams and the posts and walls carried up from them. The same system was

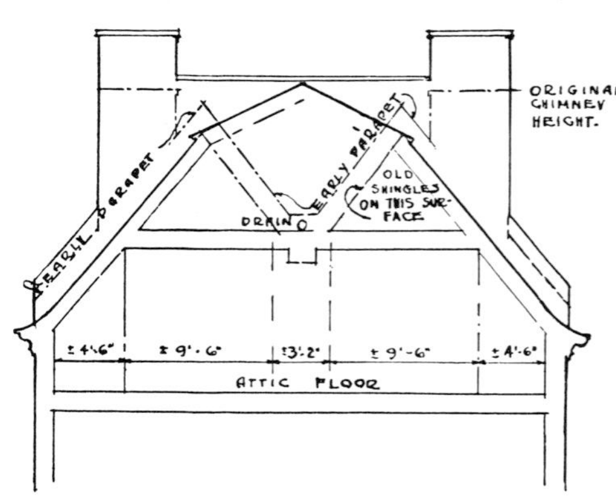

MC PHAEDRIS-WARNER HOUSE
SECTION SHOWING FIRST AND SECOND ROOFS
AND EARLY AND LATER PARAPET
AND CHIMNEY HEIGHTS.

FIGURE VI.

carried out in at least one other example in New England, the Older Bushnell house, Saybrook, Connecticut. As these sills are so wide they project well into the sides of the room and have given rise to much speculation. Tradition has it that they were intended as seats and benches and suggest a picture of the Jackson family sitting around the rooms in rows. Such is not the fact however. They are too small to have been used for this purpose and are really a structural "sport".

The first house was built at Odiorne's Point in 1623 by David Thompson, who, however, deserted it and moved to Boston on the arrival of Captain Mason's ship in 1630. It was, however, still later than this date that the first houses were built on the site of the present city of Portsmouth, which was first called Strawberry Bank. It is extraordinary to note, however, that by 1701 the various earlier forms tried in other sections with gables, casements, overhanging second stories and steep roofs had crystallized into a style and type differing from anything that had been done before, which persisted throughout the entire country and exerts a strong influence to the present day.

That this style evolved so quickly and so consistently is a wonder to all who have studied it. One of the strongest factors is the homogeneous culture and taste of the first settlers. All styles have been the result of a culture; an expression of the life of the builder, the manners and customs of the vicinity, the climate of the country, the limits imposed by the materials at hand, the traditions of the artisans employed, isolation from conflicting influences and above all a consistent and definite public taste. All of these factors were present to a remarkable extent.

The eighteenth century was a time of "form". Social etiquette was rigid, religious ideals and formalities were definite and marked, the arts and literature were carried on under well understood and carefully laid down rules. Well studied composition, balance and a fine polish were the external expressions of the thought and taste of the time. In education stress was laid on the study of the classics, and the writing of poetry formed a part of a gentleman's training. We find constant references in inventories and other records of the time to private libraries, and the publication of books well illustrated with copper engravings on architectural details, was an important branch of publishing. Not only were great volumes published on the Continent and in England, on the works of Palladio, Vignola, Vasari and other architects, dedicated to members of the aristocracy and subscribed to in advance by long lists of men of fashion and fortune but a great number of hand books and carpenters guides in a more modest form were issued with details of the orders, doors, windows, cornices, pediments and other architectural features.

The volumes noted in the following list chronologically arranged were all in use in this country, having either been imported or printed here, and give an idea of the quantity of material available at that time to the designers. We know from inventories, wills and other lists that Bulfinch, Thomas Jefferson and William Buckland owned certain copies, and their names appear in parentheses where identification is possible.

BOOKS ON ARCHITECTURE AND THE ALLIED CRAFTS USED IN AMERICA PRIOR TO 1830

Alberti, Leone Battista. Architettura del Alberti. Venetia. *1565.* L'architettura di Leonbatista Alberti; tradotta in lingua fiorentina sa Cosima Bartoli . . . con la aggiunta de' disegni. (Jefferson)

Serlio, Sebastiano. Il Settimo Libro Architettura del Serglio. Ital. Lat. fol. Il settimo libro d'architettura nel quale si tratta di molti accidenti, che possono occorer' al architetto, in duorsi luoghi, et istrane forme de siti, e nelle restauramenti, o restitutione di case . . . Francofurti ad Moenum. *1575.* Title page in Italian and Latin. (Jefferson)

Delorme, Philibert De Lorme. Invention pour batir les couvertures courbes. fol. Nouvelles pour bien bastir a petits fraiz trouvees nagueres par Philibert de L'Orme. Paris. *1576.* (Jefferson)

Scamozzi, Vincenzo. Antichita di Roma. fol. Discorsi sopra l'Antichita di Roma. Venetia. *1582.* (Jefferson)
Les Cinq Ordres d'Architecture de Scamozzi par Daviler. fol. Les cinq ordres d'architecture de Vincent Scamozzi tire du sixieme livre de son idee generale d'architecture. Par Augustin Charles d'Aviler. Paris. *1685.* (Jefferson)
Scamozzi's architecture by Leyburn. The mirror of architecture; or, the ground-rules of the art of building. Exactly laid down by Vincent Scamozzi, . . . with a description and use of the joint-rule, by John Brown . . . the 7th ed. Whereunto is added a compendium of the art of building by William Leyburn (!) London *1734.* (Jefferson)

Vignola, Giacomo Barozze, il. Regola delle cinque ordini d'architettura del Vignola. fol. Regola delle cinque ordini d'architettura del Vignola. Con la muova aggionta di Michel'angelo Buonarotti . . . Amsterdam, *1619.* See also Bibliotheque d'architecture. (Jefferson)

Rossi, Fillippo de. Ritratto di Roma Antiqua. 12 mo. Ritratto di Roma antica, nel quale sono figuratii principili tempij, teatri. Roma, *1645.* (Jefferson)

Palladio, Andrea. Palladio les 4 livres d'architecture par de Chambray. fol. The first Paris edition. *1650.* (Jefferson)
Palladio's first book on architecture, with Le Muet on doors and windows. 8vo. First book on architecture, translated out of the Italian, with an appendix touching doors and windows by Pl Le Muet, translated out of French by G. Richards. London. (*1663*) (Jefferson)
. . . 2nd edition corrected and enlarged. London. *1688.*
. . . 3rd edition. London. *1766.*
. . . 7th edition with a model of St. Paul's in London. *1708.*
. . . 12th edition. *1733.*
Palladio by Leoni. Ital. Fr. Eng. 2vo. fol. The architecture of A Palladio in four books . . . to which are added several notes and observations by Inigo Jones. . . . Revised and published by Giocomo Leoni. Translated from the Italian. . . . London. *1715.* (Jefferson)
Palladio by Leoni with Inigo Jones' notes. fol. The architecture of Palladio; in four books . . . revis'd . . . by Giocomo Leoni . . . the 3rd ed. cor. With notes and remarks of Inigo Jones. And also, an appendix containing the antiquities of Rome. Written by A. Palladio. And a

discourse of the fires of the ancients. London. *1742.* (Jefferson)

Palladio. (Venice. 1581) Reprinted London *1759.* (Bulfinch)

Palladio. les 4 livres d'architecture par de Chambray. Ie. Bibliotheque d'Architecture de Chambray. IIe partie Architecture de Palladio, contenant les cinq ordres d'architecture suivant cet auteur, ses observations sur la maniere de bien batir, et son traite des grandes chemins, et des ponts, tante de charpente que de maconnerie. Nouv. ed. Paris. *1764.* (Jefferson) See also Bibliotheque d'architecture.

Vitruvius Pollio. Abrege de Vitruve. Architecture de Vitruve reduite en abrege par Perrault. Paris. *1674* (Jefferson)

L'Architecture de Vitruve de Perrault. fol. Les dix livres d'architecture de Vitruve, corrigez et traduits nouvellement en francais avec des notes & des figures. 2nd ed. rev., cor., augm. par M. Perrault. Paris. *1684.* (Jefferson)

Donatus, Alex. Roma illustrata Donati. 4to. Roma Vetus ac Recens utriusque Aedificiis Illustrata; Amstellodami, *1695.*

Perrault, Claude. Perrault's 5 orders of architecture by James. fol. A treatise of the five orders of columns, viz., Tuscan, Doric, Ionic, Corinthian, and composite . . . to which is added a discourse concerning pilasters; and of certain abuses introduc'd into Architecture. Written in French by Claude Perrault. Made English by John James. London. *1708.* (Jefferson)

Le Clerc, Sebastien. Architecture de Le Clerc. 4to. Traites d'architecture avec des remarques et des observations tresutiles, pour les jeunes gens qui veulent s'appliquer a ce bel art. Paris. *1714.* (Jefferson)

Campbell, Colin. Vitruvius Brittanicus; or, The British Architect. London. The Author. *1715-1771* 5 vols.

Halfpenny, William. Halfpenny's practical architecture. 12mo. Practical architecture; or, a sure guide to the true working according to the rules of that science, representing the five orders . . . with their doors and windows, taken from Inigo Jones and other architects. To each plate tables containing the exact proportions of the several parts. . . . (These are the "practical" features of the book, to save calculation of exactly the same sort as Jefferson constantly made. London, *1724.* (Jefferson.)

Ditto. The 5th ed. London. Printed and sold for Thos. Bowles. *1730.*

Six new designs for convenient farmhouses . . . in brick and stone. London. Sayer. *1751.*

The second edition, with four additional designs of *Useful* architecture. London. Sayer. *1755.*

The third edition, with four additional designs of *useful* architecture. London. Sayer. *1760.*

The Carpenter's Company. Philadelphia. *1724.*

Kent, William. The architecture of Inigo Jones. *1727.*

Jones, Inigo. Inigo Jones' and Ld. Burlington's designs by Kent. fol. The designs of Inigo Jones, consisting of plans and elevations of publick and private buildings. Pub. by Wm. Kent with some additional designs. . . . London. *1727.*

Castell, Robert. Villas of the ancients. Illustrated. London. *1728.*

Morris, Robert. An essay in defense of ancient architecture. London. *1728.*

Lectures on architecture. London. *1734.*

Rural architecture. London. *1750.*

Architectural Remembrancer. London. *1751.*

Architecture Improved. *1755.*

Select architecture. *1755.* 4to. Select architecture being . . . designs of plans . . . well suited to town and country . . . from the plain town house to the stately hotel . . . from house to the parochial church . . . also bridges, baths, summer houses &c. ill. (Jefferson.)

Le Blonde, Alexander. 4to. Theory and practice of gardening; translated from the French by John James. London. *1728.* (Jefferson)

Gibbs, James. Gibbs' designs for buildings. g. fol. A book containing designs of buildings and ornaments. London. *1728.* (Jefferson, Buckland)

Gibbs' rules for drawing in Architecture. fol. Rules for drawing the several parts of architecture in a more exact and easy manner than has heretofore been practiced, by which all fractions, in dividing the principal members and their parts, are avoided. 3rd ed. London. *1753.* (Jefferson)

Langley, Batty. Langley's practical geometry (Practical geometry applied to the arts of building, surveying, etc.) London. *1729.* (Jefferson)

A sure guide to builders. London. *1729.*

The builder's complete assistant. London. *1738.*

The city and country builder's treasury of designs. London. *1740.*

Builder's Bench-mate. *1747.*

Gothic Architecture. *1747.*

Builder's Treasury. *1756.*

Ancient Architecture. *1742.*

The builder's director or benchmate; being a pocket treasury of the Grecian, Roman, and Gothic orders of architecture. London. *1767.*

Becker, W. G. The builder's dictionary. 2v. 8vo. The builder's dictionary; or, Gentleman and Architect's companion. Explaining not only the terms in art of all the several parts of architecture, but also containing the theory and practice of the various branches thereof. . . . London. *1734.* (Jefferson)

Bibliotheque d'Architecture de Iombert. 4 vols. Vignola, Scamozzi, et Chambray. *1766.* (Jefferson)

Plans d'Architecture par Becker. Neue Gärten und Landschafts-Gebaude, Leipzig. *1798.* (Jefferson)

Ware, Isaac. The four books of Palladio's architecture. *1738.*

A complete body of architecture, adorned with plans and elevations from original designs of Inigo Jones. . . . London.

T. Osborne and J. Shipton. *1756.* (Jefferson)

Designs of Inigo Jones and others. London, *1756.* (Buckland)

Hoppus, E. The gentleman's and builder's repository; or, Architecture display'd. London. Bettesworth and Hitch. *1738.*

Ficoroni, Francesco de Ficoroni. Vestigia e rarita di Roma. 4to. (Les vestigia e rarita di Roma antica. . . . Roma, *1744.*) Volume II has the title: La singolarita di Roma moderna.

Vardy, John. Some designs of Inigo Jones. London. *1744.*

Piranesi, Giovanni Batista. Varie Verdute di Roma antica e moderna. fol. Binder's title of miscellaneous plates—date of *1748.* (Jefferson)

Chippendale, Thos. The gentleman and cabinetmaker's director. London. The Author. *1745.*

Chippendale's Cabinet-Maker's Designs. fol. Gentleman and cabinetmaker's directory; being a collection of . . . designs of household furniture in the Gothic, Chinese and modern taste . . . (with) a short explanation of the five orders of architecture. . . . 3rd ed. London. *1755.* (Jefferson)

Osborne, T. English architecture; or, The Public Buildings of London and Westminster, with plans of the streets and squares, and a succinct review of their history, and a candid examination of their perfections and defects. London. For T. Osborne in Gray's Inn. 123 Plates. ca. *1755.*

Wood, Robert. Ruins of Balbec, by Wood & Dawkins. g. fol. (The ruins of Balbec, otherwise Heliopolis in Coelosyria. London. *1757.*) (Jefferson)

Swan, Thomas, Architect. A Collection of Designs in Architecture, containing New Plans and Elevations of Houses, for General Use. Printed by R. Bell, for John Norman, Architect Engraver. fol. I vol. unfin. Completed work printed in London in *1757.*

One-hundred Designs and Examples, Curiously Engraved on Sixty Copper Plates. fol. The British Architect; or the Builder's Treasury of Stair-cases. Same printer and engraver as above. *1774.* 2nd ed. *1794.* (Buckland)

Chambers, Sir Wm. Chamber's Chinese designs. g. fol. Designs of Chinese buildings, furniture, dresses, machines, and utensils, engraved by the best hands from the originals in China, by Mr. Chambers . . . to which is annexed a description of the temples, houses, gardens, etc. London, *1757.* (Jefferson)

Chamber's treatise on civil architecture, in which the principles of that art are laid down. 1st ed.—*1759.* 2nd ed.—*1768.* 3rd ed.—*1791.* 4th ed.—*1825.*

Chamber's views of Kew Gardens. g. fol. Plans, elevations, and perspective views of the gardens and buildings at Kew, in Surry, England. London. *1763.*

Le Roy, Julien David. Ruins of Athens, by Le Roy. fol. Le Roy, J. D.: Ruins of Athens, with Remains, and other Valuable Antiquities in Greece. fol. London. *1759*.

Kirby, Joshua. Kirby's perspective of architecture on Brook Taylor's principles. London. *1761*. (Wall says: *1762*.) (Jefferson) (Buckland)

Stuart, James. Ruins of Athens by Stuart and Revett. g. fol. The antiquities of Athens, measured and delineated by James Stuart . . . and Nicholas Revett. 1st vol. London. *1761*. (Wall says: *1762*.) (Jefferson) 2nd ed. London. *1825-30*.

Pain, Wm. The builder's pocket treasury; or Palladio delineated and explained. London. *1763*. Pub. by The Author.
The builder's golden rule; or, the youth's sure guide. London. The Author. *1781*. 2nd ed. *1782*.
Supplement to the Builder's Golden Rule. *1782*.
Pain's British Palladio; or, The Builder's general assistant. London. J. & J. Taylor. *1788*. (Halsey ed: *1793*.)
The practical house carpenter; or, the youth's instructor. London. The Author *1789*. (5th ed. & later ed. 1794, and 1797: Halsey.)
The practical builder; or, Workman's general assistant. 4th ed. Rev., cor., by the author, Wm. Pain, Architect and Joiner. Engraved on 83 plates. Printed and sold by John Norman. Boston. *1792*.
The builder's sketch book; or, The youth's pocket companion. London. *1794*.
The builder's pocket treasure . . . correctly engraved on 55 copper plates, . . . a new edition, London printed, Boston reprinted, and sold by Wm. Norman. *1794*.
The practical house carpenter; or, youth's instructor . . . the whole illustrated and made perfectly easy by 148 plates. The First American edition from the Fifth (see above) London Edition, with additions. Boston. Printed and sold by Wm. Norman, Bookseller and Stationer. *1796*.
Ditto. The sixth edition with additions. Philadelphia. Printed by Thomas Dobson. *1797*.
The carpenter's pocket directory. Engraved on 24 plates. Philadelphia. Published by J. H. Dobelbower & J. Thakara. *1797*.

Adam, Robert. Ruins of the Palace of the Emperor Diocletian at Spalatro. London. *1764*.
The works in architecture of Robert and James Adam. London. *1773-1822*. 3 vols.

Patte, Pierre. Monuments de Louis XV par Patte. g. fol. (Monuments erigés en France a la gloire de Louis XV) *1765*. (Jefferson)

Sanvitale, Frederigo. Elementi di Architettura del Padre Sanivitale. 4to. Brescia. *1765*.

Freart de Chambray, Roland. Bibliotheque d'Architecture Jombert. 4me. viz. Parallele de l'architecture antique et moderne par Errard et Chambray. Paris, *1766*. (Jefferson's own edition of this work may be found in the Library of Congress)

Rawlins, Thomas. Familiar architecture, consisting of designs of houses for gentlemen and tradesmen, parsonages and summer retreats. London. Printed for the author. *1768*.

Major, Thomas. Les ruines de Paestum, ou de Posidonie, dans la Grande Greece. Londres. Chez T. Major. *1768*. The ruins of Paestum, otherwise Posidonia in Magna Graecia. London. *1768*.

Swan, A. Designs for Chimney Pieces. *1768*. (Halsey)

Whately, Thomas. Observations on modern gardening, by Whately. 8vo. London. *1770*. (Jefferson)

Virloys, Roland de. Charles Francois Dictionnaire d'Architecture, Civile, Militaire, et navale. Paris. *1770-1771*.

Savery. Thomas engraved plates in Philadelphia about *1775*.

Lubersac de Livron, Charles Francois de. Lubersac sur les monuments publique. Discours sur les monuments publics de tous les ages, et de tous les peuples connus, suivis d'un description du monument projete a la gloire de Louis XVI, et de la France, par M. l'Abbe de Lubersac. Paris. *1775*.

Richardson, George. A Book of Ceilings. London. *1776*.
Treatise on the Five Orders. London. *1787*.
The New Vitruvius Brittanicus. London. *1802-1803*.

Heely, Joseph. Heely on the Gardens of Hagley. 2v. 12mo. Letters on the beauties of Hagley, Envil, and the Leasowes. London. *1777*. (Jefferson)

La Faye, Polycarpe de. De la Faye sur les chaux des Romans. 8vo. Recherches sur les preparations que les Romains donnaient a la chaux, dont ils se servoient dans leurs constructions, et sur la composition & l'emploi de leurs morties. Paris. *1777*. (Jefferson)

Soane, Sir John. Designs in architecture. London. *1778*. (Bulfinch
Plans, elevations, and sections of buildings in the counties of Norfolk, Suffolk, Yorkshire, Staffordshire, Warwickshire, Hertfordshire, etc. London. *1788*.
Sketches in architecture, containing plans and elevations of cottages, villas, and other useful buildings, with characteristic scenery. London. Taylor. *1798*.
Designs for public and private buildings. London. Priestley. *1828*.

Clerisseau, Charles Louis. Monuments de Nismes de Clerisseau. g. fol. Premiere Partie. Antiquities de la France. On cover: Monuments de Nismes. Paris. *1778*. (Jefferson)

Desgodetz, Antoine. Edifices anciennes de Rome par Desgodetz. fol. Les edifices antique de Rome, mesures et dessines tres exactement sur les lieux, par feu M. Desgodetz. Paris, *1779*. (Jefferson)

Preti, Francesco Maria. Elementi di Architettura del Preti. Venezia. *1780*. (Jefferson)

Etienne, Jean de. Etienne d'un ciment impenetrable a l'eau. (Memoire sur la decouverte d'un ciment impenetrable a l'eau. Par M. d'Etienne . . . Paris. *1782*.) (Jefferson)

Seely, B. Description of Stowe. 8vo. Description of the house and gardens at Stowe, Buckingham. *1783*. (Jefferson)

Paine, James. Plans, elevations, and sections of the noblemen and gentlemen's houses; also of stabling, bridges, public and private, temples and other garden buildings. 2 vols. London. *1783*.
James Paines' Works. Vol. I. *1767*. (Halsey)

Thomas, Wm. Original Designs in Architecture. London. *1783*. (Bulfinch)

Mascheroni, Lorenzo. Nuove ricerche sull equilibrio delle volte del Abate Mascheroni. Bergamo. *1785*. (Jefferson)

Crunden. Crunden's Original Designs. London, *1767*. 2nd ed. *1785*. (Bulfinch)

Aldrich, Henry. Elementae Architecturae Civilis. Oxford. *1789*.

Smeaton, John. Smeaton's Narrative of Eddystone Lighthouse. Narrative of the Building, and a description of the construction of the Eddystone Lighthouse. gr. fol. London. *1791*. (Jefferson)

Kersaint, Armand Guy. Discours sur les monuments publique. Par Kersaint. 4to. Paris. *1792*.

Plaw, John. Rural architecture; or, designs from the simple cottage to the decorated villa. London. *1794*.
Sketches for country houses, villas, and rural dwellings; calculated for persons of moderate income, and comfortable retirement. London. J. Taylor. *1800*.

Benjamin, Asher. Issued the first original work on architecture done in America. The Country Builder's Assistant: containing a Collection of New Designs of Carpentry and Architecture . . . correctly printed on 30 copperplates . . . printed at Greenfield (Mass.) by Thomas Dickman. *1797*.
The Same with additions. The Second Edition, printed by Spotswood and Ethridge at Worcester. *1798*.
Ditto. 3rd ed. Printed by Thos. Dickman. *1800*.
Ditto. 4th ed. Printed by John Denio. *1805*.
The American Builder's Companion; or, A new system of architecture; particularly adapted to the style of building in the United States of America. By Asher Benjamin, Architect and Carpenter, and Daniel Raynerd, Architect and Stucco Worker. Boston. Published by Ethridge and Bliss, Proprietors of the Work. S. Ethridge, Printer. Charlestown. *1806*.
Ditto. 2nd ed. Corrected and enlarged. 59 copperplate engravings. Same printer. *1811*.
Ditto. 3rd ed. Corrected and enlarged. Published by R. P. and C. Williams for the author. Printed by G. Bangs. *1816*.
Ditto. 4th ed. Corrected and enlarged. 61 copperplates. Published by R. P. and C. Williams at Boston. *1820*.
Ditto. 5th ed. *1826*.
Ditto. 6th ed. 70 copper-plates. *1826*.
The Rudiments of Architecture; being a treatise on practical geometry, on Grecian and Roman mouldings. 32

copper-plates. Boston. Printed for the author by Munroe and Francis. *1814*.
Ditto. 2nd ed. with 34 copper-plates. Published by R. P. & C. Williams. *1820*.
The practical house carpenter. Being a complete development of the Grecian orders of architecture. 64 large quarto copper-plates. Boston. Published by the author, R. P. & C. Williams, and Annin and Smith. *1830*.

Meinert, Friederich. Landbaukunst von Meinert. 4 cahiers. Schöne Landbaukunst. Leipzig. *1798*. (Jefferson)

Atwood, G. A. A Dissertation on the Construction and Properties of Arches. London. *1801*. (Bulfinch)

Mitchell, Robert. Mitchell's Perspectives of Buildings in Engl'd, Scotl'd. gr. fol. Fr. Eng. Plans and views in perspective, with descriptions of buildings in England and Scotland, and an essay on Grecian, Roman, and Gothic Architecture. London. *1801*. (Jefferson)

Krafft, Johann Carl. Plans des maisons de Paris par Krafft et Ransonnette. fol. Plans, Forms, Elevations of the Most Remarkable Houses and Hotels erected in Paris and its Environs. In English, French, and German. Paris. *1801-02*. (Jefferson)

Norman, William. The Builder's Easy Guide; or, Young Carpenter's Assistant: containing a great variety of useful designs in Carpentry and Architecture. . . . To which is added a list of the price of the Carpenter's Work, in the town of Boston. Printed by W. N. Boston. *1803*.

Biddle, Owen. The Young Carpenter's Assistant; or, A system of Architecture adapted to the new style of building in the United States. By Owen Biddle, House Carpenter, and Teacher of architectural drawing. Philadelphia. Printed and sold by Benjamin Johnson. *1805*.
Ditto. Published by Johnson and Warner. . . . Philadelphia. Printed by Robert and William Carr. 2nd ed. *1810*.
Ditto. Printed by Wm. Brown. *1815*.
Ditto. Published by Benjamin Warner. Philadelphia. Printed by William Dickson, Lancaster, Pa. *1817*.

Gyfford, E. Designs for elegant cottages and small villas . . . to which is annexed a general estimate of the probable expense attending the execution of each design. London. J. Taylor. *1806*.

Johnson, Stephen William. (Brewer) Rural Economy: Containing a treatise on Buildings; . . . on the culture of the vine; and on turnpike roads. With 8 plates. New Brunswick, N. J. Printed by William Elliot. For I. Riley & Co. New York. *1806*.

Haviland, John. The Builder's Assistant, containing the five orders of architecture. 150 copper-plates. By John Haviland, Architect, and engraved by Hugh Bridport, Artist. Vol. I (II & III) Philadelphia. Published by John Bioren. . . . *1818-1824*.
A description of Haviland's Design for the New Penitentiary, now erecting near Philadelphia. Published by Robert DeSilver. *1821*.
The Practical Builder's Assistant . . . 150 Engravings. 2nd ed. Baltimore. F. Lucas Jr. *1830*.
A description of Tremont House, with architectural illustrations. Boston. Published by Gray and Bowen. *1830*.

Nicholson, Peter. The Carpenter's New Guide; being a complete book of lines for carpentry and joinery . . . 84 copperplates. The eighth edition from the sixth London edition. Philadelphia. Printed and Published by M. Carey & Sons. Griggs & Co. Printers. *1818*.
Editions of this book were printed after *1830*.

Mitford, William. Mitford's Principles of Architecture. 8vo. Principles of designs in architecture traced in observations on buildings primeval, Egyptian, Phoenician . . . in a series of letters. . . . London, *1819*. (Jefferson)
Second Edition. *1824*.

Pocock, William Fuller. Designs for churches and chapels, of various dimensions and styles; consisting of plans, elevations, and sections, with estimates. A new edition. London. J. Taylor. *1824*.

Louden, John Claudius. An encyclopedia of cottage, farm, and villa architecture and furniture. London. Longman. *1836*.
An encyclopedia of gardening. 4th ed. London, Longman. *1826*.

Lafever, Minard. The Young Builder's General Instructor; containing the five orders of architecture . . . 66 elegant copper-plate engravings. By Minard Lafever, Architect and Practical Builder in the City of New York. Newark, N. J. Printed by W. Tuttle & Co. *1829*.

Milizio, Francesco. Principi di Architettura Civile dal Milizia. 3 vol. 8 vo. (Principi di architettura civile. 3rd ed. rev. emend. ed accresciuta di figure da G. B. Cipriani. Bassano. *1830*.)

Of these books, the works of Asher Benjamin, Batty Langley, William Kent, Thomas Swan, William Pain and Robert Adam were most used in this section. That they were extensively used may be seen by comparing the designs of these books with the executed work. One may find in these volumes the original designs from which doors and door trims, windows, cornices, mantel pieces, details of stairways, and other architectural motives, as well as details of framing and construction were copied. Sometimes they were exactly reproduced but more often some slight variation was given by the individual craftsman. In Swan, published in London, 1745, Plate XXIII, one finds a design for a doorway with Doric frieze and columns similar to the treatment in the Jewett House where it was made into a porch instead of a frontispiece treatment. In William Kent's book on the work of Inigo Jones, published in London, 1727 on Plate LV figure 5 is a frieze ornament of barbaric birds ending in foliated scrolls, similar to the frieze ornament of the main entrance door of the Lady Pepperrell house and the frieze of the mantel piece of the Governor John Wentworth house except that a central shell has been omitted and the scrolls reversed. Judging by the technique of the carving and the similarity of these two ornaments they were done by the same carver.

The general types of plan are few, but slight variations to meet the individual requirements of the family were made so that no two plans are exactly alike. The earliest type contained on the first floor one room and an entry which usually faced South, behind the entry a large chimney and between that and the entry or porch a small, steep stairway. The second floor was similar. (Figure II).

The second type was made by adding a fireplace and a second room on the other side of the entry both to the first and second floors, making a four room house with four fireplaces, the great chimney, which was of massive construction being placed in the middle of the house. (Figure III).

The third type was made by adding at the rear or North side three more rooms to the first story and continuing the rear slant of the roof of the second story down to the eaves of the first forming a lean-to extension. At first this extension was usually added to the four room type of house as may be seen by the additions and patching out of the original framing in many surviving examples, but later it became an integral part of the original plan

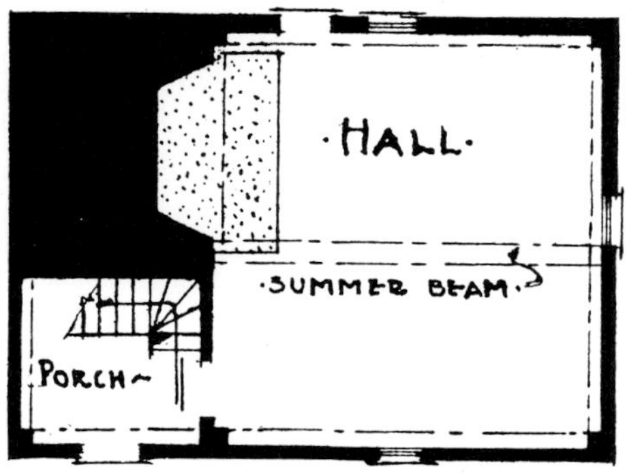

·First·Floor·Plan·

·House of Typical One Room Plan·
One and a half or two stories high~
·Figure II·

and was erected at the same time as the rest of the house. The center room at the rear with a large fireplace and oven was used as a kitchen. One small room at the corner sometimes being used as a buttery and the other corner room which often opened off the kitchen being used as a bedroom. (Figure IV). The Col. Paul Wentworth House, 1701, (page 131), is of this type. That the lean-to was a later addition to this house is clearly seen in the "lean-to" flues added at the back of the central chimney and the closing up of the rear window of the panelled or West chamber on the second story.

The final and fourth development of the single, central chimney type was made by adding three more rooms to the second floor, on the rear, directly above the kitchen, buttery and bedroom, with a second stairway usually leading up from the kitchen. The large room above the kitchen was called the "Kitchen Chamber" and small rooms at the side of it corresponded to the buttery and bedroom below. This type of house contained ten rooms, four of which were without any means of heating and two of these could only be entered by passing through another room.

Often a one story wing or "ell" was added to these types which contained a second chimney and, continuing from this, in farm houses, sheds, a barn, and other service parts were added in a long line so that stock could be attended to in cold and bad weather without having to go out of doors, particularly important at times of heavy snow storms.

A central hall was then introduced extending from the front to the rear, giving better ventilation and direct access to all the rooms. There are many examples of plan where two units of the two room house were placed at either side of the hall (Figure V), and later the chimneys were placed on the end walls giving better access from room to room. The plan of Lady Pepperrell's house shown on page 10 is an early example of this plan, which with variations became more used than any other. North and South in early houses and houses of the Early Federal Period one may find countless examples. Sitting rooms, "parlours", bedrooms and the dining room flanked the central hall while the kitchen and other service rooms were placed in the ell. When, to this house plan, a second stairway was added, according to the definition of the popular building hand books, the house was raised to the dignity of a "Mansion".

An early house illustrating this type of plan is the Macpheadris-Warner house put up between the years 1717 to 1725. Built of brick its various stages of development throw much light upon our early methods of procedure in construction. The house as it stands today differs in many ways from its original design. The accompanying measured drawing of the section, Figure VI, taken through the roof shows the design of the original roof which strangely enough is still standing beneath the present roof in fairly complete form even to some of the original shingles on the inner sides. This roof was similar to the Tudor double gable roof used in England on the old type of building until that time, with two long ridges running parallel to the long front with a valley and wide gutter between. The figure in broken line shows this outline, the original height of the chimneys and the outline of the original brick parapets. A circular hole in each end wall led the roof water from the central gutter down a leader, the slots for which may still be seen in the belt courses. The figure in full line shows how this roof was later decked over and the chimneys and copings raised. While a roof like this in England with lead plate and flashings would be fairly tight when kept in constant repair, in this severe climate with heavy snows filling up the deep pocket, with shingles as the only protection against melting snow-water, and with the scarcity of metal for flashings it is most probable that the roof leaked badly in heavy rains and at times of melting snow. No signs of metal flashing can be found nor even the holes of the nails which held it can be identified. As metal flashing was little used, many buildings at this early period being put up without any even around the chimneys, it is possible that none was installed and on account of the leaks it was decked over above the two ridges to form the more fashionable and modern gambrel roof.

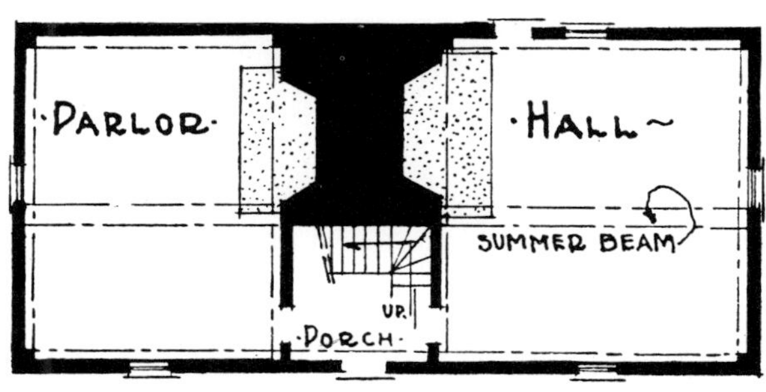

·First Floor Plan·

House of Typical Two Room Plan
·Figure·III·

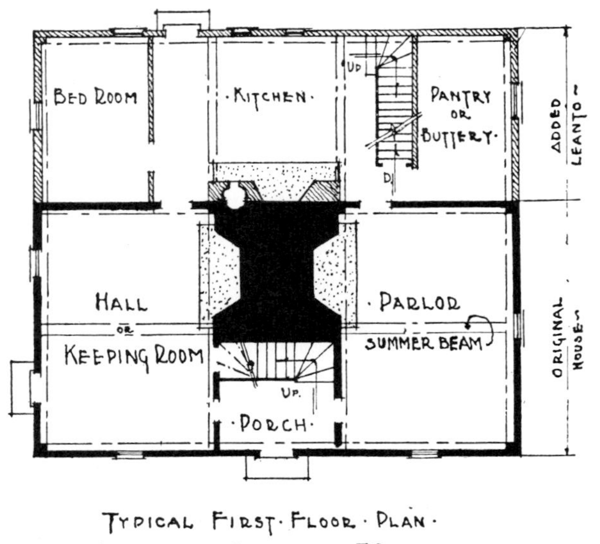

Typical · First · Floor · Plan ·
· Central Chimney Type ·
· Figure IV

In the rear room at the left of the hall is one of the largest fireplaces in Portsmouth. It appears to be an ordinary sized fireplace with a Dutch oven at one side very much as shown in the kitchen in figure IV, but investigation discloses that this later fireplace and oven had been built into the great original fireplace and the original pine sheathing in this same room is buried under a later finish of lath and plaster.

Of the types discussed so far the buildings were limited to either one or two stories with an attic; with various forms of wings or ells, usually built on at the rear and one or two stories high. Five windows on the second floor across the front with a central entrance door flanked by two windows on either side on the first floor was the almost invariable rule. In the South and particularly from Maryland southward, where more space was required, flanking buildings were added, sometimes entirely disconnected, sometimes connected by hyphen-wings, arches or open roofed passages. Care was taken to make them symmetrical and with the balance of mass, roofs, and chimneys, a great variety of interesting forms was evolved. In New England, however, with few exceptions, such as the Governor Gore house at Waltham, Mass., 1804-1806 or the Col. John Black house at Ellsworth, Maine, built in the early XIXth century, balancing symmetrical wings flanking the main body of the house were rare.

The three story house which is an important type is better represented in Portsmouth than in any other city. It was so much used that on Middle Street, Brewster states that for a long distance on one side there was only one two story house. They existed in other towns but as a rarity. There are actual records here of at least fifty-five, and of these no less than thirty are illustrated in this volume. As wealth and families increased it became necessary to enlarge the house, and it was increased in size upward rather than laterally. On account of the coldness of the climate it was more practical from the point of view of the heating to continue the compact plan upward and place additional bedrooms in the third floor. The disconnected and exposed flanking wings used in the south would have been too difficult to heat. Economy in construction was another important factor, for the high square house required less foundation walls and less roofing than the extended plan and economy was one of the salient virtues of New England.

Owing to the lack of space in the towns and the importance of limiting the house site area in the country to the smallest convenient dimensions, in order to use the land for productive farming purposes, a small yard was all that was permitted at the entrance side. Extensive gardens, distant views and important landscape designs, such as are found in the South, are the exception and not the rule. Hamilton House, with its beautiful site at South Berwick, Maine, and the Moffatt-Ladd house in Portsmouth with its terraced and shady gardens are notable exceptions. This restraint in the use of land for the house site is another reason for the development of the three story house.

The most important reason for the development of the three story house is found in the character and ideals of these early builders. Desiring a fairly balanced and formal type, and within the rigid outlines prescribed by custom, no variation in design was considered desirable. A vivid imagination in aesthetic matters was not a characteristic of this community and conventional standards, rather than experiments in design were the rule.

About 1750 Charles Treadwell built the three story house standing on the South-east corner of Congress and Middle Streets now called the Cutter house, for his son, Jacob. It was later bought by Dr. Ammi R. Cutter whose descendants still occupy it.

Nearly square in plan the house has a central hall, a hip roof and two chimneys. The wooden quoins on the corners in imitation of stone design, the fine cornice, the

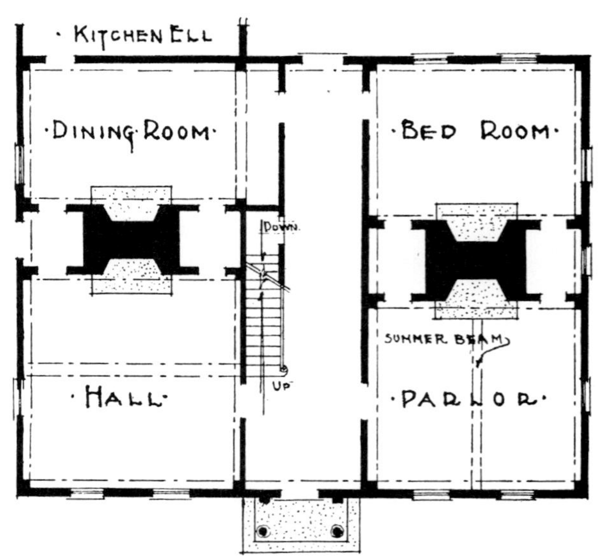

Typical First Floor Plan ·
· Central Hall Type ·
· Figure V ·

beautifully executed bonnet hoods and pediments on the windows together with the fine interior woodwork are eloquent of the rapid advance in building and design. This house, built within a century of the early simple houses, is perhaps the earliest three story house now standing, although as early as 1735 Samuel Sherborne built one near the Alms House at Christian Shore, which is now destroyed.

The Moffatt-Ladd house on the West side of Market Street was built in 1763 by Captain John Moffatt, (born in Hertfordshire, England in 1692—died 1786), for his son Samuel Cutt Moffatt. Captain Moffatt came to this country in command of one of the King's mastships when the masts were loaded at Kittery Point. He married Catherine Cutt, daughter of Robert Cutt 2nd, of an important Portsmouth family, settled in Portsmouth and had a numerous family. He soon became a prosperous merchant, an importer, and the head of a counting house. His son, Samuel Cutt Moffatt graduated from Harvard University in 1758, married Sarah Catherine Mason and shortly after occupied this house so elegant and so large that it was the wonder of the town. It is a three story house, has four chimneys, a steep hip roof, a handsome staircase, that occupies a front corner of the house, a large wing connected to stables adjoining a picturesque courtyard, and at one side a separate one story counting house. The gardens which are terraced, and graded, are among the most beautiful of the old gardens in New England.

About 1800 Langley Boardman, an expert cabinet maker built the house known by his name on the West side of Middle Street. The simplest and at the same time the most beautiful of all the houses of this type at Portsmouth, the designer evidently had in mind to carry out a facade such as had already been done many times, substituting flush ship-matched planking for the clapboarding or brick elsewhere used, and at the same time greatly beautifying his design by the charming proportions, attenuation and refinement of the columns and pilasters of the curved porch with its beautiful doorway, and the Palladian window motive above. The contrast in the squareness of the third story windows to the greater height of those of the first and second stories, the well marked main cornice giving relief to the plain surface of the wall and the delicate but strong design of the central motif, make a design distinguished, restrained and interesting.

Here one may see the type of Palladian window often used by the Adam Brothers and the restraint of the style of the English Regency but all fused by perfectly studied relationships and proportions into an original and perfect whole. Such delicacy of moulding treatment and fineness of design as are here shown would hardly be consistent with the heavier material and the larger scale of a brick building, but as it is, this house remains perhaps the most beautiful, chaste and distinguished instance of the Puritan treatment of this type of dwelling to be found in the New England Colonies and should serve as epilogue and apogee of the development of colonial dwellings unique and restricted to this section of North America.

The profession of architect as practiced today is very different from that of the architectural designers of the XVIIIth century. It is true that Minard Lefever in New York in 1829, and John Haviland in Philadelphia in 1818, styled themselves Architects in publishing their books, but one of the first and few men who assumed the professional status in limiting his work to preparing plans and specifications and supervising the work, which was carried out by others, was Gabriel Manigault who practiced architecture in Charleston, S. C. in 1790. One may get an intimate and detailed view of the status of an architect of that time by examining the will and its accompanying inventory of William Buckland of Anne Arundel County, Maryland. He was the son of a carpenter, the nephew of James Buckland, a book-shop proprietor in London to whom he was apprenticed in 1745 for seven years. One can see the young man poring over the architectural volumes of his uncle, collecting notes, sketches and books, and noting the architecture of the great houses he saw himself, such as Honington Hall near Oxford where he lived for some time. In 1755 he was made an indentured servant to Thomson Mason, brother of John Mason, for four years, at twenty pounds American a year, came to this country and helped him in designing and erecting Gunstan Hall in Fairfax County, Virginia. After serving his time he settled in Annapolis, designed a number of important houses, among others the Chase, Harwood-Hammond, probably Whitehall and a number of others. He prospered greatly, married, and died in 1774, rich for those times, respected and the owner of considerable property. His daughter married John Callahan, Register of the Land Office, and his grand-daughter, Sarah Callahan, married Richard Harwood, who owned the house that Buckland built for Matthias Hammond. Buckland's splendid portrait by Charles Wilson Peale still hangs there.

His will lists his possessions of certain "Goods and Chattels" and seriously sets forth:—

Thomas Waits *a Man Servant and Bricklayer*	20	0	0
John Tintton *ditto ditto*	20	0	0
Samuel Baily *a Carpenter and Joiner*	16	0	0
Michael Burke *a Painter*	10	0	0
James Reynolds *a Carver*	16	0	0
Lawrence Oherr	2	10	0
Oxford *a Negro Man*	60	0	0
Sue *a Negro Woman*	25	0	0
Hannah *a Young Negrowoman*	50	0	0
Joe *a Negro Boy*	15	0	0
Beck *a Negro Girl*	12	0	0
3 Chefts Carpenter Tools	15	0	0

One Cheſt Carvers ditto	1	0	0
Two Cows	5	0	0
One Mahogany Deſk and Book Caſe	12	0	0
One ditto Dining Table	2	8	0
One ditto Tea ditto	1	4	0
One Walnut Cheſt of Drawers	2	0	0
And ſo forth			

Further down one finds Tools, Building Materials:

Old Lumber conſiſting of Carpenters Old Tools etc.	1	0	0
Four Trowels 1 Lathing Hammer and 2 Old Spades	0	4	0
77 Squiares of Glass in a Box 11 by 9 @ 8d	2	11	4
33 Cheſnut Poſts for Pailing	1	2	0
45 three Square Railed Bails @ 10/ per hundred	0	2	6
491 Cleft ditto @ 18/ per ditto	4	8	4½
557 Cleft Pail Boards @ 20/ per thouſand	0	11	1½
046 lbs Glue	2	6	0
630 Feet of 1½ Inch Pine Plank @ 8/ per hundred	2	10	4¾
960 Feet of Old Plank uppon the Scaffolds and lying in and about the Building 4/	1	18	4¾
400 Feet of Old Pine Scantling laying about the Lotts and Building much damaged 6/	1	4	0
30 Buſhels Hair @ 16d	2	0	0
180 lbs 4d Nails	2	8	10
320 lbs 30d ditto	6	12	0
45 lbs 10d ditto	9	1	2
3500 Bricks	3	10	0
60 Buſhels Lime	1	0	0
2 ornamented Ceilings of Paper	10	0	0
1 large white Picture Frame	2	0	0
2 Ladders 5/—2 Pannelled Doors 16/	1	1	6
3 Ballend Doors	0	12	0

Among his Books on Architectural Deſign and Ornament one notes:—

WARES DESIGNS	2	0	0
GIBBS DESIGNS	2	0	0
SWANS BRITISH TREASURY	0	8	0
SWANS ARCHITECT	0	12	0
THE LONDON ART	0	1	0
LANGLEYS DESIGNS	0	10	0
CHIPPENDALES DESIGNS	0	6	0
KIRBYS PROSPECTIVE *2 Vol*	1	0	0
LIGHTHOLDERS DESIGNS	0	8	0
LANGLEYS *Gothic Architecture*	0	6	0
Eſſay on ditto	0	4	0
JOHNSONS CARVERS *Deſigns* (*Thomas Johnſon London 1761*)	0	2	0
HOPPUS MEASURER	0	1	0
SWANS CARPENTER INSTRUCTOR	0	4	0
MORRIS DESIGNS	0	1	0

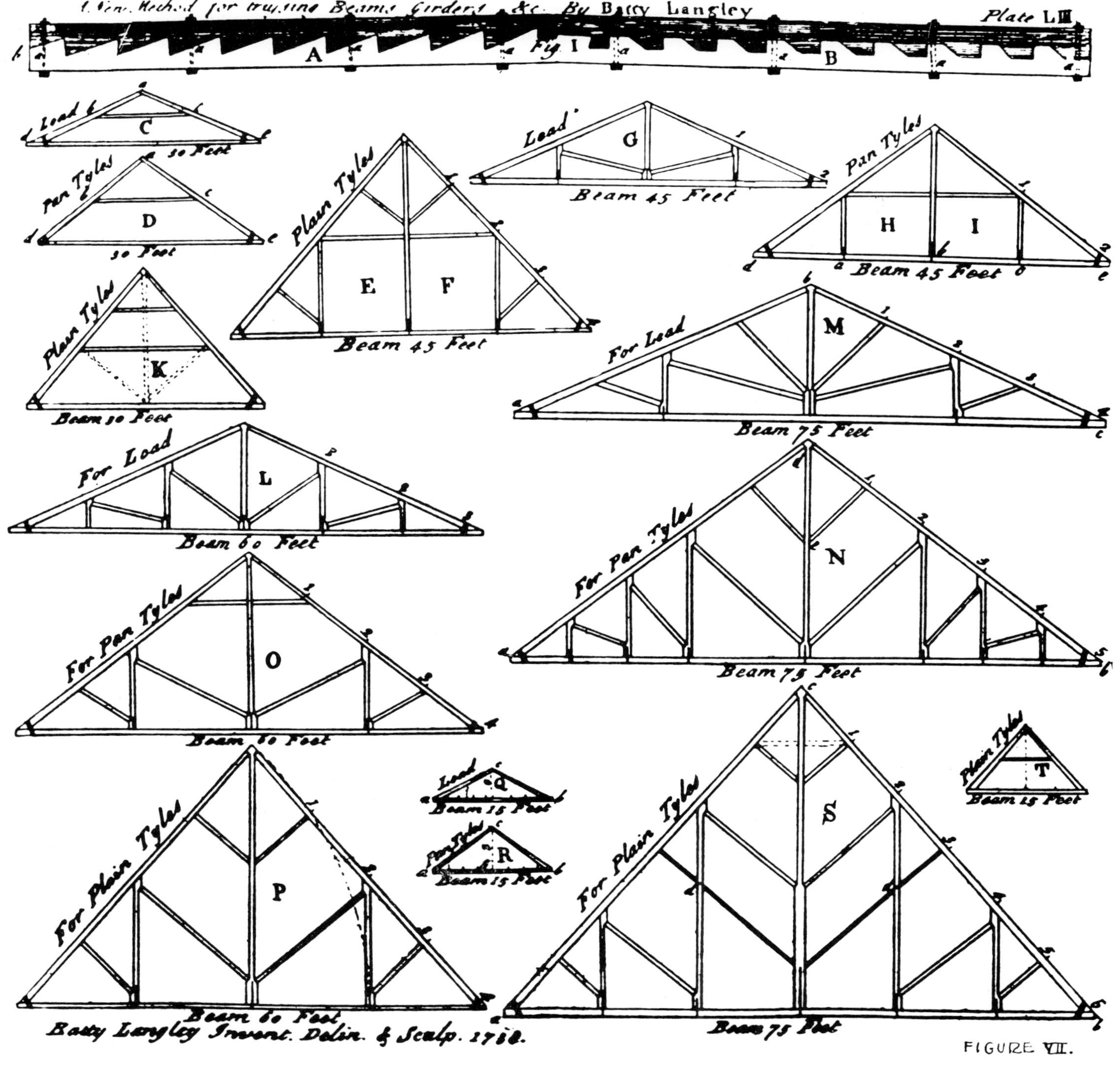

FIGURE VII.

Thus we see that Buckland not only designed the buildings but kept a stock on hand of timber, bricks, ornamented papier-mache ceilings, compo ornament, carved mirror and picture frames and furniture.

The same practice was universal to a greater or lesser degree throughout the country. Sometimes an artisan would be a carpenter, and mason, a carpenter and plasterer, a cabinet maker and carpenter, but more often carried on only one of the building trades. Many men had most diverse interests and combined shipping and importing with tannery and operating sawmills, doing a little speculating in land and trading in horses and cattle on the side.

The prospective house builder would decide on the size and type of house he wished, choose a combination of workmen and lay out the building, frequently directly on the site without the formality of any drawings and merely a few notes on sizes. All the workmen collaborated in the erection of the building and worked according to their trade rules and personal experience. When it came time to decide about the framing of the roof truss, for instance, reference might be made to a plate in

THE

BUILDERS Compleat ASSISTANT,

OR, A

LIBRARY

OF

ARTS and SCIENCES,

Abſolutely Neceſſary to be underſtood by

BUILDERS and WORKMEN in general.

by **B. Langley**, above referred to, as for instance Plate LII in Volume II. (Figure VII). The prices for labor, carpenters prices, materials such as shingles, clapboards and "nayles" were regulated by local ordinances and published in books. Mr. Alexander J. Wall has found copies and references to such books and has listed a number of them including House Carpenter's Books of Prices, and Cabinet Makers Price books. These indicate that the principal cities, Philadelphia, New York, New Haven and Boston had each its society of tradesmen which published "Rules of Work" that specified the amount to be charged for all work. Of these, four were published in Philadelphia in 1786, 1801, 1806, and 1827, one in Carlisle, Pa. in 1796, one in New York in 1817 and two in Boston in 1774 and 1880.

In a small community like Portsmouth everyone knew what everyone was doing, and one may imagine how the straight bottom step with curved side and balustrade of which we may find numerous examples in the Pepperrell, and other early houses, received much favorable notice, as it was copied so many times. The oval panel under the stair soffit was also much admired and whoever the plasterer was who originated this beautiful detail, he evidently executed it three times in the Moffat Ladd, the Gov. Langdon, and the Col. Whipple houses.

Thus we have seen that many factors have contributed to the development of the methods of design and construction of the buildings of our early days. Much data remains still unexamined and further investigation should throw further light on how our American style came about. In getting these facts together I have had the help and suggestion of that kind and versatile scholar Mr. R. T. H. Halsey and have drawn freely from the valuable works of research of Mr. Fiske Kimball, Mr. J. Frederick Kelly and Mr. Alexander Wall, and to all of them I wish to make my grateful acknowledgments:

William Lawrence Bottomley

NEW YORK, OCT. 1937

THE ARCHITECTURAL HERITAGE OF THE PISCATAQUA

THE GOVERNOR LANGDON HOUSE—1784—
Portsmouth, N. H.

The similarity of architectural treatment of this splendid house, and of Hamilton House in South Berwick, allowing that they were built about ten years apart, suggests the same designer or architect. A wing was added to this house, in 1906, by McKim, Mead & White.

This mansion was built in 1784 by Governor John Langdon, and was occupied by him. He was, with Captain Pickering, John Sullivan and others, engaged in the seizure of the powder at Fort William and Mary in December, 1774. His cousin, Samuel Langdon, afterward conveyed part of this powder to the army at Cambridge, and it was used in the battle of Bunker Hill. In 1878 this same cousin Samuel conducted two loads of clothing to Washington's suffering army at Valley Forge—the gift of the inhabitants of Portsmouth.

Mr. Langdon was chosen Governor of New Hampshire. While he was Speaker of the House of Representatives, convened at Exeter in 1777, he rose and made the following declaration, which will ever enshrine his memory in the hearts of the sons of New Hampshire: "I have a thousand dollars in hard money. I will pledge my plate for three thousand more. I have seventy hogshead of Tobago rum, which will be sold for the most they will bring. They are at the service of the State. If we succeed in defending our firesides and our homes, I may be remunerated; if we do not, then the property will be of no value to me."

He was the first President of the United States Senate, and, there being neither President nor Vice-President, he was for the time Acting President, and as such informed General Washington of his election. He entertained Louis-Philippe and his brothers at this house; and here Washington dined several times with Mr. Langdon, when here in 1789, and recorded it as the handsomest house in Portsmouth. The small brick lodges in front are a unique feature; similar ones were in front of his brother's house before the Rockingham was rebuilt. In 1782 the Marquis de Chastellux wrote: "After dinner we went to drink tea with Mr. Langdon. He is a handsome man and of noble carriage. His house is elegant and well furnished and the apartments well wainscoted." Mrs. Woodbury Langdon, the present owner, is a great great granddaughter of the builder.

Fig. 1

Governor Langdon House—Front View

Fig. 2

Governor Langdon House—Great Chimney Place in North Drawing Room

Fig. 3

Governor Langdon House

This house is a magnificent example of the fully developed early American architecture. Both interior and exterior show the mastery which our builders, joiners and carvers had achieved over their materials. Such a house is popularly called a "Colonial Mansion", and as such, is dear to the hearts of Americans.

Fig. 4

Governor Langdon House—Stair Hall

Fig. 5

Governor Langdon House—South Drawing Room

LADY PEPPERRELL HOUSE—CIRCA 1760—
Kittery Point, Maine

This house was built sometime soon after 1759 for Lady Pepperrell, widow of Sir William Pepperrell, the hero of Louisburg. He was the only American baronet. Until 1759 the Pepperrells resided in the old Pepperrell mansion built by Sir William's father in the late 1600's, shown in plate 166 of this book. Sir William was called "The Pascataway Trader" and was considered the richest man in the colonies; his wealth was estimated at 250,000 sterling. In 1745 he was named Commander in Chief of the Louisburg Expedition for which he raised and financed a regiment. In recognition of his success at Louisburg he was received in London and given a baronet age by the King.

Architects will notice how heavily the window trim, caps and sills project outside of weatherboarding. This throws the whole window to the outside of the wall and gives inside shutter embrasures and window seats in a frame house.

The broad front walk of white and dark beach stones laid in patterns was found under heavy turf.

The almost universal difficulty of getting correct the spelling of the Pepperrell name, may be dispelled by the following verses published at one time by Judge Shaw of Kittery:

Would writers learn to rightly spell
The ancient name of Pepperrell?
Just as the Baronet, of old,
Once wrote it out in letters bold?
Then please these easy lines recite,
And one will surely have it right:

Of letters four, make ten from these—
Of p's and r's and l's and e's;
Begin with P and e, and then—
Use all the letters that you can;
That is to say, in Pepperrell,
Use doubles p and r and l.

Justin Henry Shaw

Fig. 6

LADY PEPPERELL HOUSE

The side piazzas were added by a recent purchaser. Such piazzas were popular additions to older houses just before and after the Revolution. Mr. Fiske Kimball cites a letter from the painter Copley to Henry Pelham who was looking after the erection of Copley's house in Boston, asking him to be sure to add the then fashionable "peazer" to his new house.

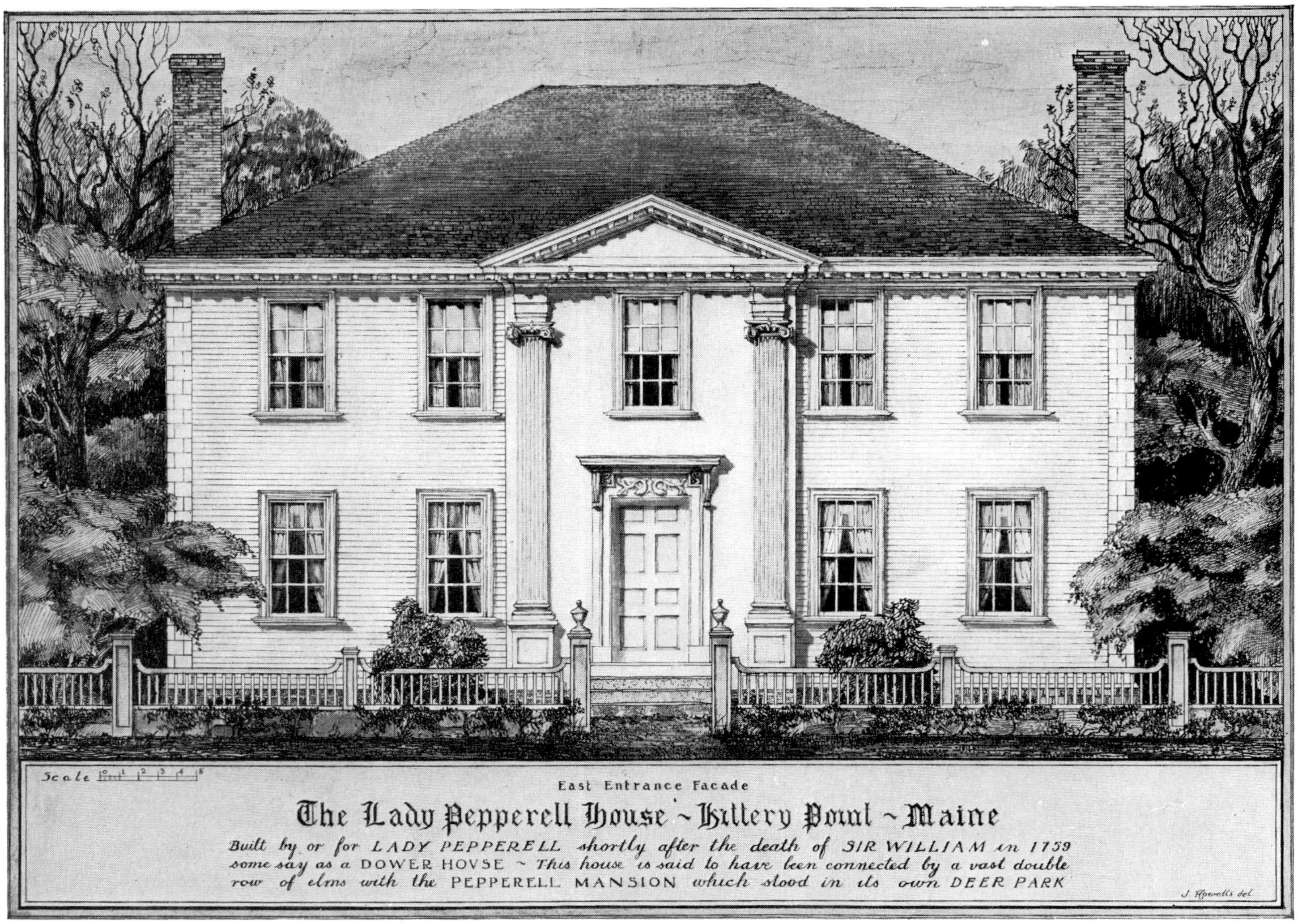

Scale 0 1 2 3 4 5

East Entrance Facade

The Lady Pepperell House ~ Kittery Point ~ Maine

Built by or for LADY PEPPERELL shortly after the death of SIR WILLIAM in 1759 some say as a DOWER HOVSE ~ This house is said to have been connected by a vast double row of elms with the PEPPERELL MANSION which stood in its own DEER PARK

J. Howells del.

Fig. 7

Fig. 8

Lady Pepperrell House—Front View

Fig. 9

Lady Pepperrell House—A Bedroom

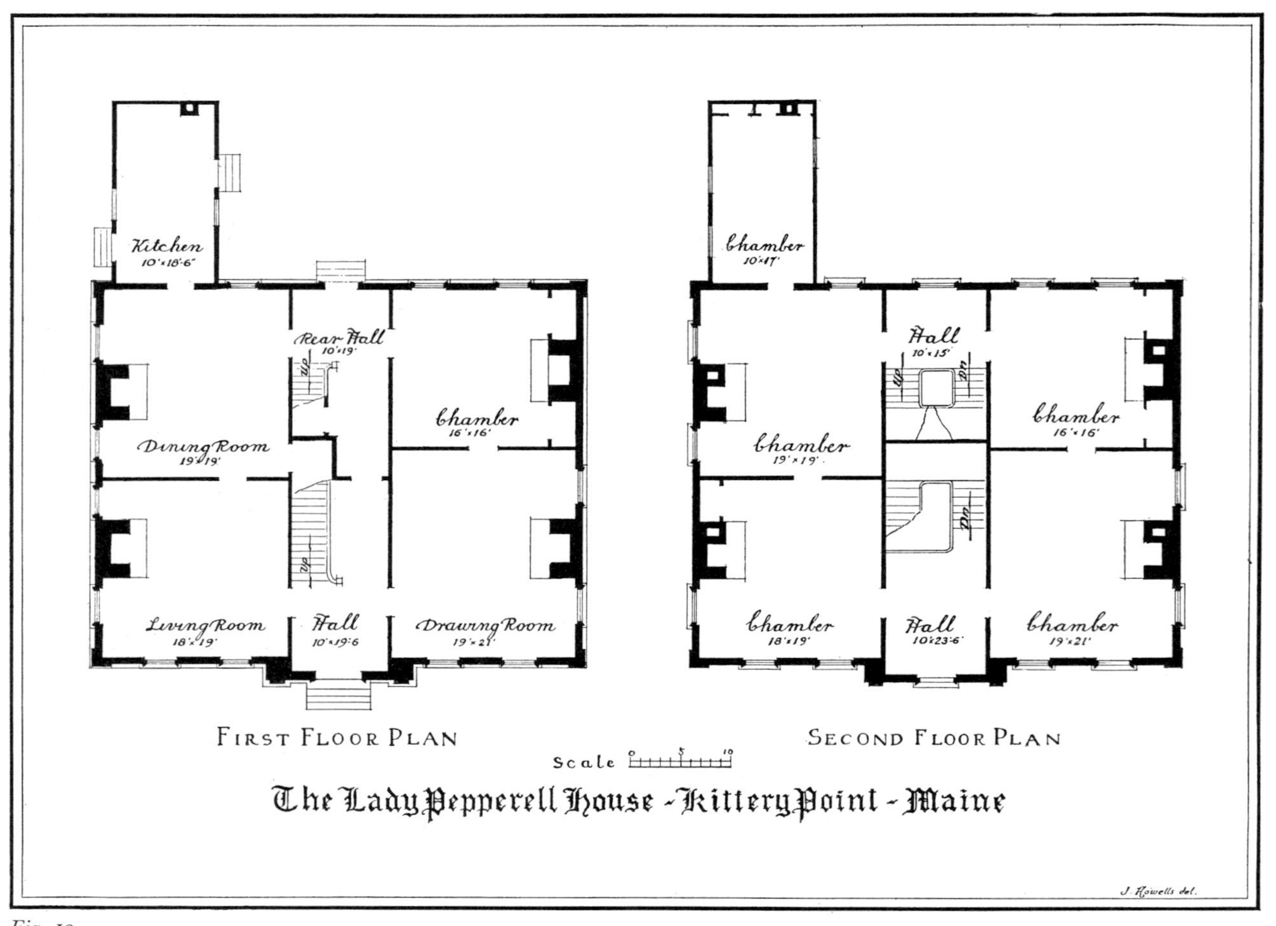

Fig. 10

Fig. 11

Lady Pepperrell House—North Drawing Room

Fig. 12

Lady Pepperrell House—Dining Room

Fig. 13

Lady Pepperrell House—Upper Stair Landing with a piece of the original wall paper

Fig. 14

LADY PEPPERRELL HOUSE—MAIN STAIRWAY

This shows the openwork newel post carved from the block and typical of the ship carvers of this coast.

MACPHEADRIS—WARNER HOUSE
1712-15 (Gurney) 1718-23 (Brewster,
Daniel Street, Portsmouth

This is the oldest brick house in Portsmouth and has been described as the "earliest mansion in New England." It was built at a cost of 6000 pounds—a vast sum for those days, by Captain Archibald Macpheadris, who came from Scotland. He married Sarah Wentworth, one of the sixteen children of Lieutenant Gov. Wentworth, and their daughter married Hon. Jonathan Warner, a member of his Majesty's Council until the Revolution.

Of Warner, Brewster writes—"We well recollect Mr. W. as one of the last of the 'cocked hats.' As a vision of early childhood he is still before us, in all the dignity of the aristocratic crown officers. That broad back, long skirted brown coat, those small-clothes and silk stockings—those silver buckles and that cane, we see them still, although the life that filled them ceased fifty years ago."

The claim is made that the brick and some other material used in the construction of the house was brought from Holland, but it is more likely that here, as in so many cases where this claim is made, the brick was of the type known in the trade as "Holland Brick" from its size and shape, and may have been so billed. The original bills, and bills of lading for the furniture and plate, dated 1716, are still in the possession of the family. Bricks were also used for underpinning extending considerably below the surface.

An astonishing fact is that the old gambrel roof is not the original roof. Before that, there were double peaked roofs running the whole length of the building, with a deep valley between them. Inside the great gambrel roof can still be seen the outer surfaces of the first roofs, with the shingles still in place.

Such double parallel roofs can still be seen in England, and one can only suppose that the snow and ice made this impossible in Portsmouth.

Fig. 15

MACPHEADRIS-WARNER HOUSE—VIEW FROM STREET

Fig. 16

MACPHEADRIS-WARNER HOUSE—FRONT DOOR AND ENTRANCE MOTIF

The large brass door handle has a protective trick. The door cannot be unlatched until the handle and escutcheon-plate have been slid upwards.

Fig. 17

MACPHEADRIS-WARNER HOUSE—STAIR LANDING AND FRESCOED FIGURES

Says Brewster:—"At the head of the stairs on the broad space each side of the hall windows, there are pictures of two Indians, life size, highly decorated, and executed by a skillful artist. These pictures have always been on view there, and are supposed to represent some with whom the original owner traded in furs, in which business he was also engaged. Not long since, the front entry underwent repairs. There had accumulated four coatings of paper. In one place on removing the under coating, the picture of the hoof of a horse was discovered. This led to further investigation—the horse of life-size was developed, and a little further work exhumed Gov. Phipps on his charger. The next discovery was that of a lady at a spinning wheel (ladies spun in those times) who seems interrupted in her work by a hawk lighting among the chickens. Then came a scripture scene. Abraham offering up Isaac—the angel, the ram, etc. No person living had any knowledge of the hidden paintings—they were as novel to an old lady of eighty, who had been familiar with the house since her childhood, as to her granddaughter who discovered the horse's foot."

This house is provided with a lightning rod, which was put up in 1762 under the personal inspection of Doctor Benjamin Franklin and was probably the first in New Hampshire.

Fireplace Surround
Door Architrave
Panel Mould
Cornice
Dado Cap
Base
Elevation of North Wall
Details of Parlor
McPhedris-Warner House
PORTSMOUTH • • NEW • HAMPSHIRE
Graphic Scale
Elevation
Details
Actual Scale
Elevation 1/4" = 1'-0"
Details 1½" = 1'-0"
Francis T. King del

Fig. 18

Scullery
12 x 18
Kitchen
13½ x 14½ x 10¾
Chamber
11¾ x 13 x 10¾
Dining Room
15½ x 16 x 10¾
Hall
9¾ x 33 x 10¾
Parlor
18 x 19½ x 10¾
First Floor Plan

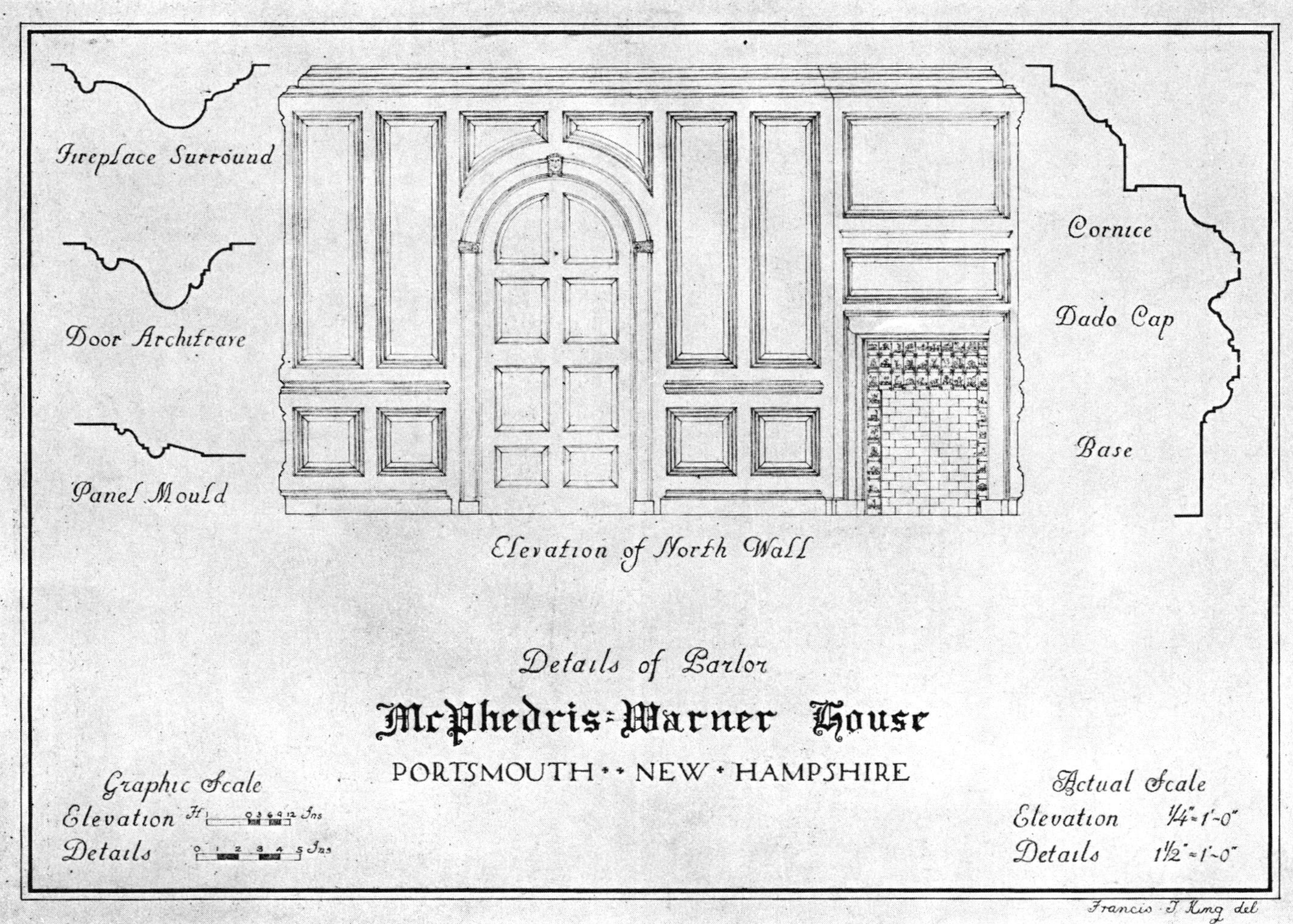

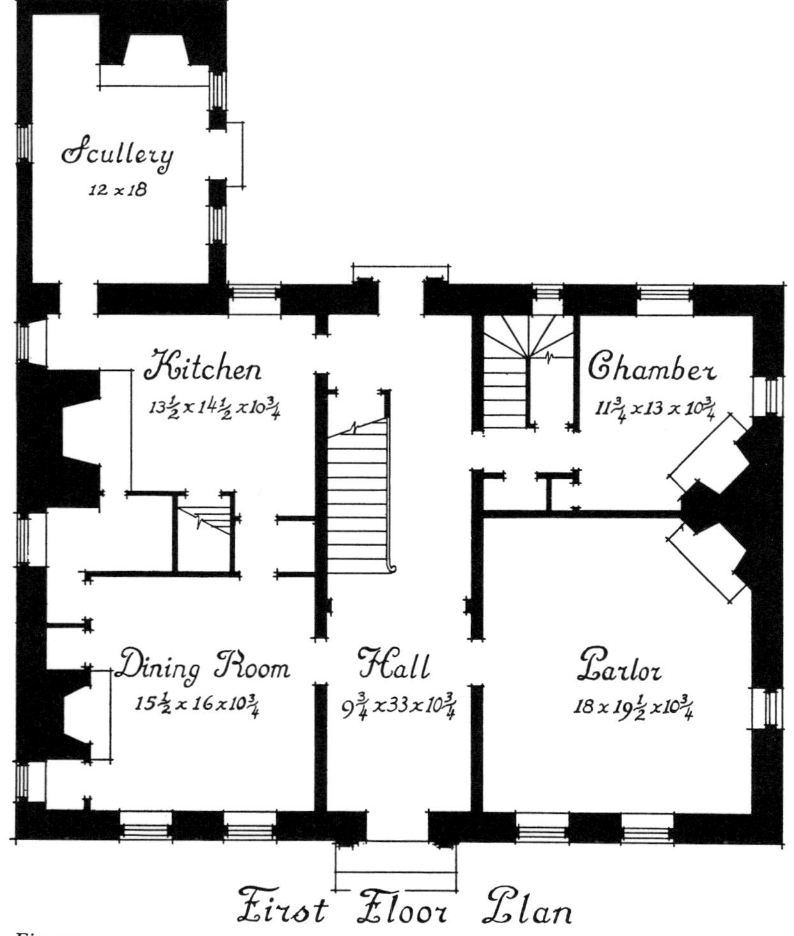

Fig. 19

Fig. 20

Macpheadris-Warner House—Stair Hall

Fig. 21

Macpheadris-Warner House—Panelling in East Front Room

GOVERNOR JOHN WENTWORTH HOUSE
CIRCA 1769
Between Pleasant Street and the South Pond, Portsmouth

Built about 1769, for the last Royal Governor, John Wentworth, son of Mark Hunking Wentworth, and nephew of Benning Wentworth. Governor John Wentworth was born in 1736, and received his commission as Governor, succeeding Governor Wentworth, in 1767. At the beginning of the Revolution he was the Royal Governor, and consequently defended the Crown, while at the same time his father and uncle were active participants in the patriot cause.

In 1775 a Royalist named Fenton, a former captain in the English Army, and a recent member of the Exeter convention, took refuge at the Governor's residence. A mob gathered before the house, and demanded that he be given up and taken to Exeter for trial. This was done, and the Governor, deeming it an insult to himself, left the house, it is said, by the back way, through his garden, to the South Pond, where he boarded a boat and was taken to Fort William and Mary, where he sought protection, while the mob entered and ransacked the house. In one of the front rooms a broken marble chimney-piece is yet to be seen, kept there as a memento of the attack. Governor Wentworth afterward went to England, where he was created Baronet, and appointed Governor of Nova Scotia in 1792, where he died in 1820. The family portraits of the Wentworths, by Copley and his master, Blackburn, were once preserved in this mansion. His large stable, in which he kept sixteen horses for family use, was opposite, on the present site of the house of William J. Fraser.

Fig. 22

Governor John Wentworth House—Gate and Entrance Doorway

Fig. 23

GOVERNOR JOHN WENTWORTH HOUSE—FRONT VIEW

Fig. 24

Governor John Wentworth House—Stair Hall

Note the scalloped base board against wall to correspond to treads and risers.

Note lower step very much elongated, also that all balusters are of same pattern, and not in triplets as is often the case—also that newel is the same pattern enlarged.

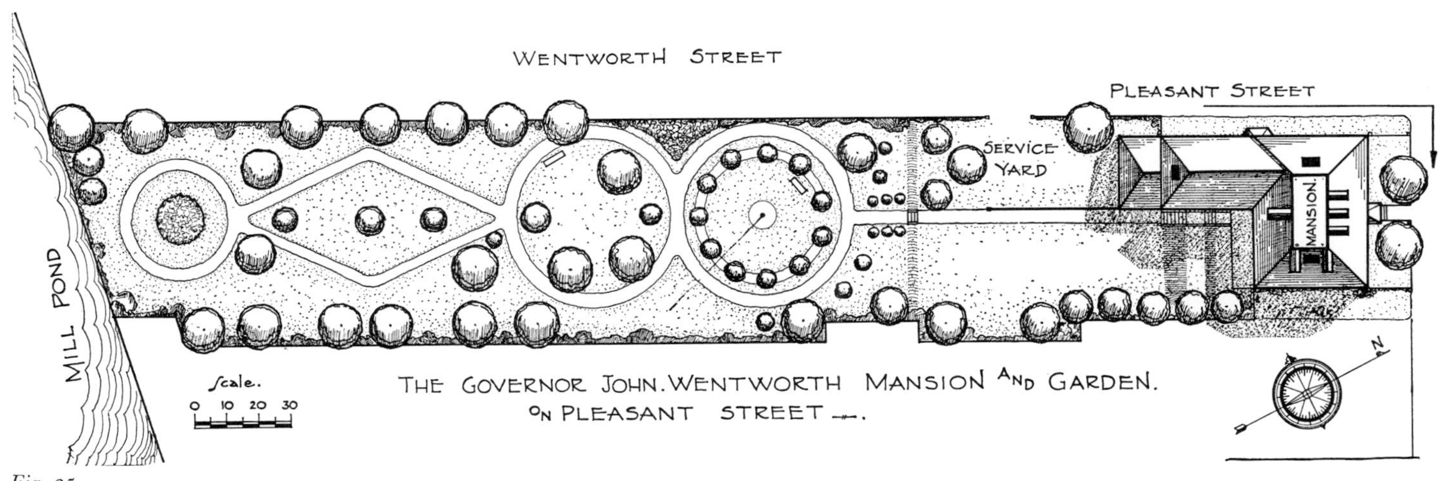

Fig. 25

Fig. 26

GOVERNOR JOHN WENTWORTH HOUSE—ORIGINAL MANTEL

Note the pattern of reversed dolphins—so much like the same motif above the front door of Lady Pepperrell House at Kittery Point, (Fig. 27) as to suggest, or almost to assure, the same carver. These houses were built within a few years of each other.

Fig. 27

THE PEIRCE MANSION—1799—
HAYMARKET SQUARE
PORTSMOUTH

THE PEIRCE MANSION—1799—
Haymarket Square
Portsmouth

While most of the Portsmouth residences are referred to in local histories as this or that "house"—this truly superb old building seems to be automatically called the "Peirce Mansion"—and really its stateliness and the beauty of its emplacement make this seem natural.

In 1799 John Peirce built the magnificent mansion at Haymarket Square, and was considered a little crazy for building a town house on the outskirts of the town. The house has earmarks of being the work of Charles Bulfinch, architect, who is believed to have designed a number of buildings in Portsmouth. Since 1799 the house has been in the Peirce family and is today occupied by Winslow Peirce, great grandson of the builder.

The owners have told this writer that they have, to date, (1937) found no documents proving Bulfinch as its designer. It seems, however, entirely possible, even probable, that he may have been. The treatment of the lovely façade is closely in the same spirit as the Sears House in Mt. Vernon Street in Boston, and of the Ezekiel Hersey Derby House (now destroyed) in Salem. Both of these houses were by Bulfinch.

Fig. 28

THE PEIRCE MANSION—FRONT VIEW

Fig. 29

THE PEIRCE MANSION—DOORWAY IN HALL

The fluted piers without capitals and the general plainness give a similarity to certain modernistic work.

Fig. 30

THE PEIRCE MANSION—STAIRCASE

Whoever designed this house, probably designed and had built the mahogany settle which is made to fit the curve of the stairs.

The present owners describe the weapons as the duelling swords of an ancestor—either the builder or earlier.

The entrance leading under the soffit of the stairs is a clever piece of design.

Fig. 31

THE PEIRCE MANSION—DRAWING-ROOMS

Fig. 32

THE PEIRCE MANSION—DINING ROOM

Notice the fine furniture in both these plates, in keeping with the settle in the stair hall.

MOFFATT—LADD HOUSE—1763—
Portsmouth

Built in 1763 by John Moffatt as a present for his son Samuel. Capt. John Moffatt was born in England in 1692. He was commander of one of the King's mast ships, which loaded masts for the King's Navy in Pepperell Cove, Kittery Point. He settled in Portsmouth, becoming a very rich man, and married the daughter of Robert Cutt of Kittery, and granddaughter of John Cutt, the first President of New Hampshire. The son, Samuel, also made a great deal of money, but failed in business in 1768, left the country, and acquired another fortune in the West Indies, where he died in 1780. On his failure, his father purchased the house that he had built, and lived in it until he died, in 1786. It passed finally into the hands of Samuel's granddaughter, Mrs. Alexander Ladd. It is still owned by the Ladd family, and has been given, through a lease at a nominal charge, to the New Hampshire Society of the Colonial Dames of America, who have furnished and preserved it and its garden in true Colonial fashion.

Adjoining the house is the separate "office" in which the gentlemen of the family carried on their shipping business. As the long mast-house is across the road on the shore, it seems probable that the shore front was for business and never beautified. On the other hand, the great gardens rise in terraces behind the house and are apparently disposed today as in Colonial times. Unaltered Colonial gardens are rarer than Colonial houses.

In the plan of this house, and also the Joseph Whipple house, the staircase is given more than half the front of the house, creating a great "Hall" in the English sense.

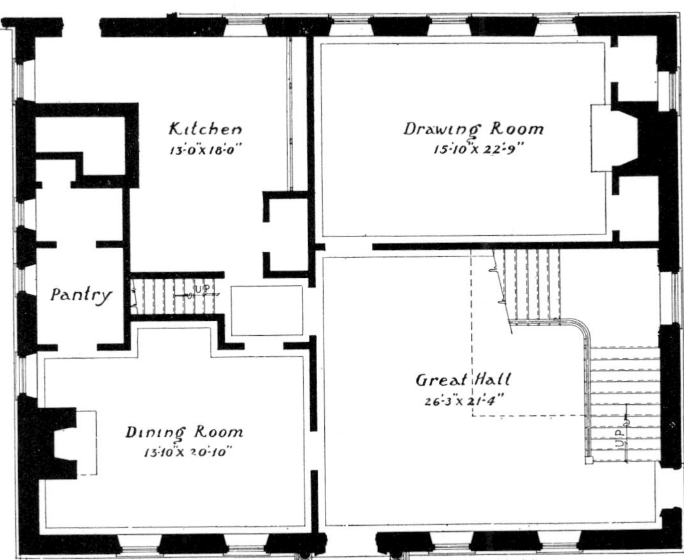

Fig. 33

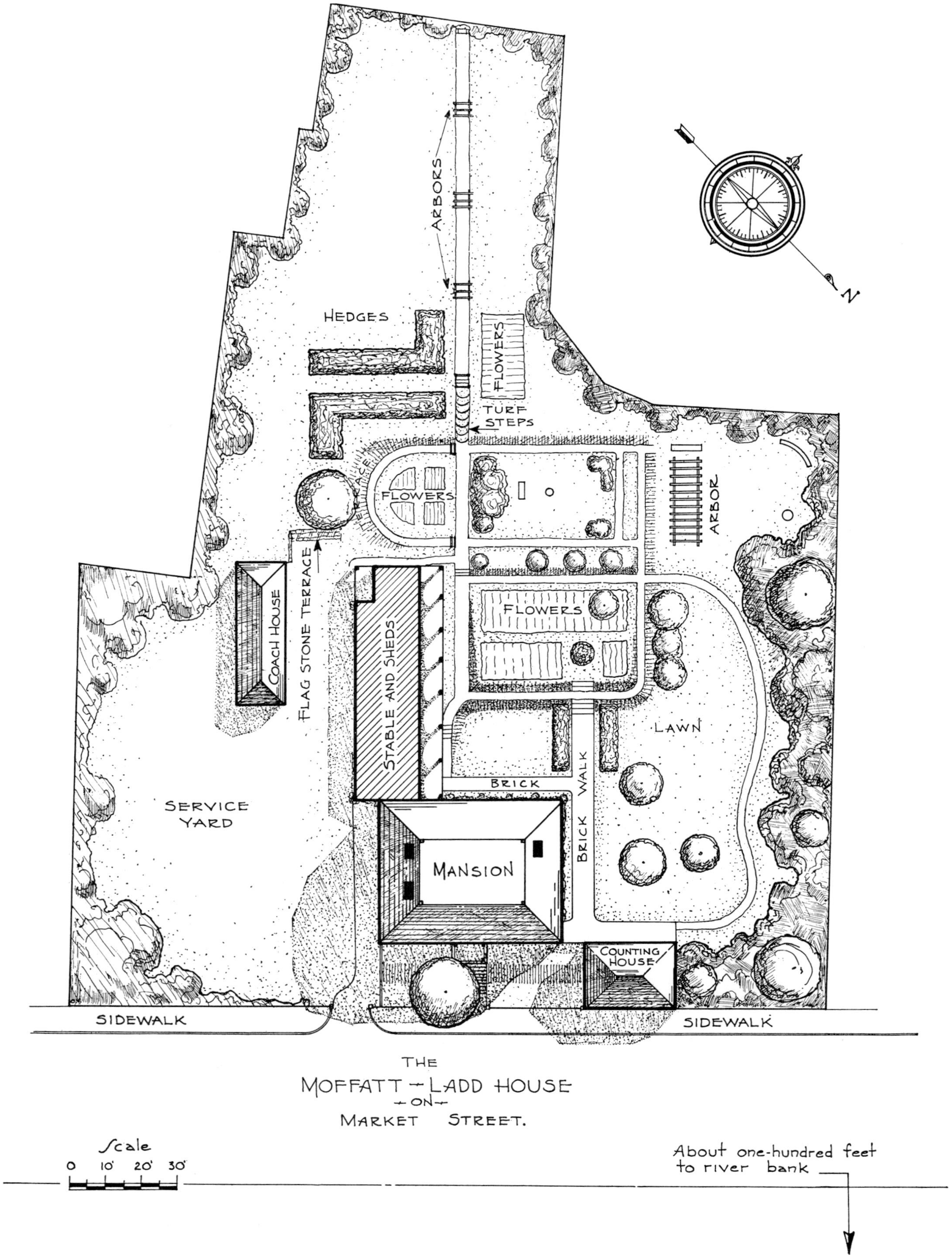

ARBORS
HEDGES
FLOWERS
TURF STEPS
TERRACE
FLOWERS
ARBOR
FLAG STONE TERRACE
COACH HOUSE
STABLE AND SHEDS
FLOWERS
LAWN
BRICK
BRICK WALK
SERVICE YARD
MANSION
COUNTING HOUSE
SIDEWALK
SIDEWALK
N
THE
MOFFATT — LADD HOUSE
— ON —
MARKET STREET.
Scale
0 10' 20' 30'
About one-hundred feet to river bank

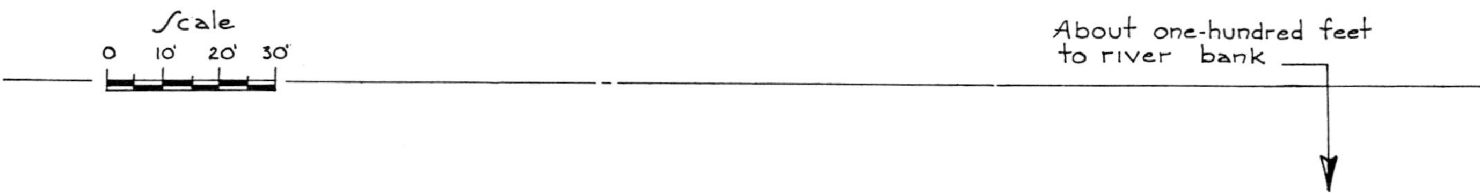

Fig. 34

Fig. 35

MOFFATT-LADD HOUSE—FRONT VIEW

Fig. 36

MOFFATT-LADD HOUSE—GARDENS

These splendid Colonial gardens, rising in terraces, are coeval with the house—a rare example in New England. This path shows the masonry steps below and the turf steps above.

Fig. 37

MOFFATT-LADD HOUSE—GARDENS

Looking back on the center axis towards the house, under an arch of rose vines.

Fig. 38

Moffatt-Ladd House—Mantel in Dining Room with original tile facing.

Fig. 39

Moffatt-Ladd House—Great Stair Hall

This is one of the few instances—one of the two in Portsmouth—where more than half the floor space of the front of the house is given to the great stair hall, as in the earlier English work.

Fig. 40

Moffatt-Ladd House—Drawing Room Mantel

This is the drawing room mantel known as the "Grinling Gibbons Mantel." There is apparently no proof that it is from his hand.

SPARHAWK HALL—Circa 1740—
Kittery Point, Maine

The fine gambrel roofed mansion was built by Sir William Pepperell for his daughter at the time of her marriage to Nathaniel Sparhawk, which took place in 1742. This must date the house just prior to that time.

It is, and was intended to be, a truly baronial hall, with a splendid hallway and ballroom, running the full depth of the house, a feature much commoner in the South, than in New England. The old English pronunciation of Sparhawk like "Sparruck"—persists, though in the hall there hangs today the carving of a hawk perched on a spar.

Fig. 41

Sparhawk Hall—Entrance door

Fig. 42

Sparhawk Hall—General View

Fig. 43

Sparhawk Hall—Banquet Room on Ground Floor

Fig. 44

Sparhawk Hall—Cupboard on Chimney Splays in Banquet Room

COLONEL JOSEPH WHIPPLE HOUSE
Circa 1760
Portsmouth

Joseph Whipple was the son of Capt. William and Mary (Cutts) Whipple of Kittery, Me. He was born in the Whipple garrison at Locke's Cove, Feb. 14, 1737. While his brother William was seeking his fortune on the seas, Joseph was employed in the Counting Rooms of Mr. Nathaniel Carter of Newburyport, Mass. For some time before the outbreak of the Revolution, the Whipple brothers were in business in Portsmouth, their place of business being on Spring Hill. The Messrs. Whipple became prosperous merchants; Joseph being the most successful of the two because he was a natural financier. In 1763 Joseph Whipple married Miss Hannah Billings of Boston and the couple took up their residence in this charming house, which Joseph probably built. In 1784 President Weare appointed Mr. Whipple a colonel in the historic Twenty-fifth Regiment of New Hampshire Militia. After the Revolution Col. Whipple received the appointment of Collector of the Port of Portsmouth, which he kept, with the exception of a few months, until his death in 1816. He transacted the business connected with this office in the small building adjoining his house, which is interesting, as showing that this was part of the original design.

Col. Whipple was the proprietor of great tracts of land in the north country, in the towns of Colebrook, Jefferson and Bretton Woods. In fact, he was one of the pioneer settlers of the White Mountain district. He built a large country house at Jefferson, N. H. and spent much of his time there dealing in lumber, which was a lucrative business. Although he was away from Portsmouth many months at a time, he always kept his town house, which was one of the loveliest in Portsmouth, and still is considered one of the finer houses of the town.

Fig. 45

Colonel Joseph Whipple House—General Exterior View

Fig. 46

COLONEL JOSEPH WHIPPLE HOUSE—UPPER PART OF STAIR

Fig. 47

COLONEL JOSEPH WHIPPLE HOUSE—OLD COACH YARD

The yard is paved with irregular fitted granite slabs, like the opus incertum of the Romans. Entrance is directly from the street.

Fig. 48

Colonel Joseph Whipple House—Upper Stair Hall

Fig. 49

Colonel Joseph Whipple House—Lower Stair Hall

This is the second of the two examples in Portsmouth where much of the front of the house is given up to a great stair hall.

Fig. 50

Colonel Joseph Whipple House—Garden Front looking across Coach Yard

HAMILTON HOUSE—1770—1775
South Berwick, Maine

These rolling acres, overlooking the tide-water, were owned as early as 1639 by one Richard Nason and by his family for generations. This charming house was built by Col. Jonathan Hamilton, a prosperous West India merchant, the son of Joseph Hamilton of South Berwick. Jonathan Hamilton was born in 1745, and married Miss Mary Manning of Portsmouth, N. H., February 8, 1771. Many of the scenes of Miss Sarah Orne Jewett's historical romance, "The Tory Lover," took place in and about Hamilton House. Col. Hamilton and his lovely daughter entertained Capt. John Paul Jones at dinner at this house on the eve of his departure for France bearing news of the surrender of Burgoyne.

In after years the old house fell into a state of decay, and was a very sad object when it was purchased in 1899 by the mother of the present owner, Mrs. Henry Vaughan, who carefully restored it to its former glory.

This house resembles in several architectural features, the Gov. Langdon House, shown at the beginning of this book. The dormer windows are peculiar and alike. There was originally a roof balustrade or whalewalk on each, and the drawing room chimney-breasts, set between recessed arches, are alike in treatment.

Fig. 51

HAMILTON HOUSE—FRONT VIEW FROM THE LAWN

Fig. 52

HAMILTON HOUSE—LOOKING UP FROM NEAR THE WATER

This view shows the beautiful location of the house on a high point of land. Vessels of early days could lie at anchor in front of the house.

Fig. 53

Hamilton House—Carriage Entrance Front

There is little level land on the point where the great house stands.

Fig. 54

HAMILTON HOUSE—GREAT DRAWING ROOM

Fig. 55

HAMILTON HOUSE—ENTRANCE HALL, ARCH AND STAIR

Fig. 56

Hamilton House—Landing and Upper Stair Hall

Fig. 57

Sally Hart House—date unknown

This tiny house was removed from Newington in 1906. It was set up in the north garden of the Hamilton House.

JACOB WENDELL HOUSE—1789
Portsmouth

Built in 1789 by Jeremiah Hill and purchased in 1815 by Jacob Wendell. The house was beautifully furnished by its new owner with all the appointments of the time. The American Chippendale furniture is said to have been bought at the sale of Sir John Wentworth's effects during the Revolution, (by John Wendell) and was inherited by his son Jacob Wendell.

On entering the house one is instantly taken back a hundred and fifty years. Everything which confronts the eye not only represents a typical example of a gentleman's house of the beginning of the 19th Century, but in most instances has been undisturbed for a long period of time. Since 1815 almost nothing has been purchased for the house, but, due to its continuous occupation by one family, pieces of family furniture have come, from time to time, to take their places beside the possessions of the original owner. There has been no division of the furnishings.

The old hall is wainscoted waist-high, and hung with the ancient fire-buckets of the Friendly Fire Society. The staircase is designed with an entresol, or mezzanine story, which speaks volumes for the taste of the builders of that early day in the opportunity afforded, not alone for commodious access to the upper stories, but also for raising the height of the rooms there located. The interior, therefore, presents a picture, rare today in America beyond the formal precincts of a Museum, of a house still occupied in comfort and privacy by the descendants of the man who first made it his home.

Fig. 58

JACOB WENDELL HOUSE—GENERAL EXTERIOR VIEW

Fig. 59

Jacob Wendell House—Coach-House

Note the unique arched opening worked under a single pitch roof.

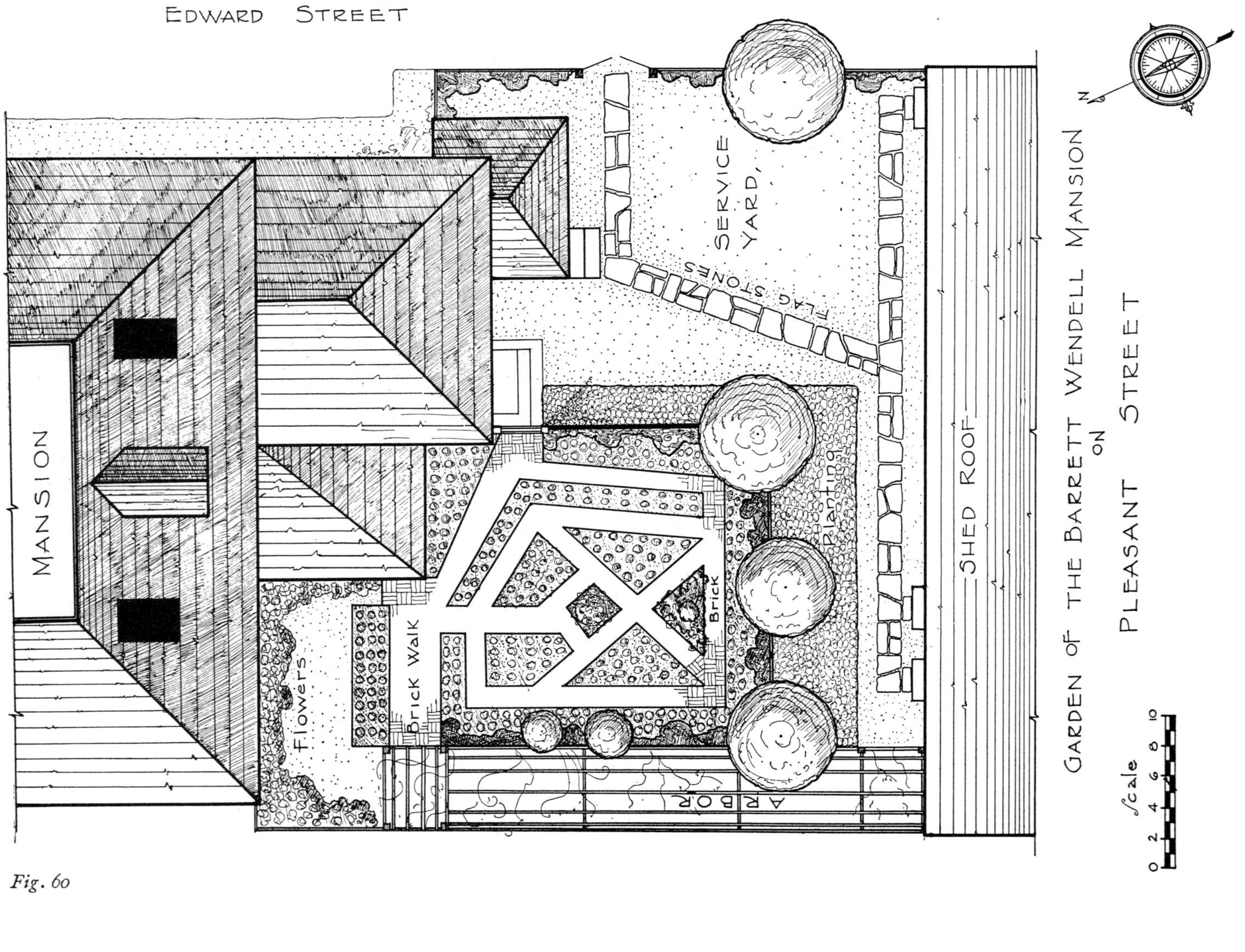

Edward Street

Service Yard

Flag Stones

Mansion

Brick Walk

Flowers

Brick

Planting

Shed Roof

Arbor

Garden of the Barrett Wendell Mansion on Pleasant Street

Scale 0 2 4 6 8 10

Fig. 60

Fig. 61

Jacob Wendell House—Stair Hall

Gurney admired the mezzanine treatment by which the chambers are reached from the stair landing by steps to the right and left.

LANGLEY BOARDMAN—MARVIN HOUSE—Circa 1800
Portsmouth

Langley Boardman, a cabinet-maker by trade, was the builder of this house. His advertisement in the New Hampshire Gazette, August 4, 1798 reads as follows: "Langley Boardman respectfully informs his friends and the public that he carries on the cabinet-makers business at his shop in Ladd Street in all its various branches." Langley Boardman was at one time a Senator in the New Hampshire legislature.

One of the most interesting features is the elliptical staircase which winds gracefully from the first to the third floor of the house. The wall covering of the hall is a pictured paper depicting Scott's "Lady of the Lake."

Of this paper Gurney says it was put there in 1816. But the Encyclopedia Brittanica, 14th edition, shows two reproductions of this paper with the following note: "Wall paper in grey and sepia, painted by Jean Zuber of Rixheim, Alsace, circa 1830, representing scenes from Scott's "Lady of the Lake."

The present owner, who bought the house in 1900, says that he then talked with an old man, still a paper-hanger, who told him that he had himself assisted as a boy apprentice in hanging this paper in this house, at some time about 1840.

The singular front door with the oval panels edged with whalebone, the delicate elliptical stair, and the perfect door heads in the style of McIntire of the neighboring town of Salem, all make it interesting to conjecture whether Langley Boardman, himself a prominent cabinet-maker, did not have some hand in the design and execution of these details. Stephen Decatur, in fact, in his article on Boardman, published in 1937, says frankly, "He probably designed his own house."

Architects have spoken of this house as a perfect example of the town type of early American house. Much dignity and beauty is gained from the smooth stone-like surface of the matched boarding of the front.

Fig. 62

Langley Boardman-Marvin House—General Exterior

Fig. 63

LANGLEY BOARDMAN-MARVIN HOUSE—DRAWING ROOM MANTELPIECE

This mantelpiece is spoken of as being by McIntire and certainly it is strikingly like the Drawing Room mantel in the Pingree House in Salem, by him, even to the leaf enwrapped composite columns.

Fig. 64

LANGLEY BOARDMAN-MARVIN HOUSE—ELLIPTICAL STAIRWAY LOOKING UPWARDS

Fig. 65

LANGLEY BOARDMAN-MARVIN HOUSE—ELLIPTICAL STAIRWAY

Fine in scale and of great beauty

Fig. 66

LANGLEY BOARDMAN-MARVIN HOUSE—LOOKING ACROSS ENTRANCE HALL

There is just a glimpse of the precious unspoiled original wall paper illustrating Scott's "Lady of the Lake"—also of the door heads which certainly suggest McIntire in treatment.

Fig. 67

LANGLEY BOARDMAN-MARVIN HOUSE—LOOKING FROM THE STAIR HALL

The inside transom has two painted glass panels and there may have been more originally.

LARKIN-RICE HOUSE—1815
Portsmouth

Built in 1815 by Samuel Larkin, who had amassed a fortune as auctioneer for English vessels taken by Portsmouth privateers. There were more than twelve of these commissioned privateersmen out of Portsmouth, and they brought rich prizes into the harbor. Mr. Larkin and his wife had twenty-two children, and shortly after their house was finished they found themselves not in a position to keep up such an establishment, and returned to their "white house" next door. A rather pathetic entry in Mr. Larkin's diary, Aug. 31, 1829, reads—"This day I moved (back) into the house from which I moved in 1817, having lived in the brick house almost twelve years."

This house is one of several Portsmouth buildings claimed by tradition to be by the architect Charles Bulfinch—but there are no documents in these cases. There is in this instance, however, a sort of coincidence. The writer has only once before noted the singular window treatment, which is identical with the Burd House in Philadelphia long since destroyed, of which a photograph is shown by Fiske Kimball in his invaluable book*. That house was by Latrobe who preceded Bulfinch as architect of the Capitol at Washington. Bulfinch admired Latrobe's work and must have been familiar with the Burd House. Bulfinch was in practice until after 1830 when his Augusta, Maine, State House was built, so the date of this house would admit the possibility of his having been its architect.

* Domestic Architecture of the American Colonies and of the Early Republic.

Fig. 68

Larkin-Rice House—General Exterior View

Fig. 69

Larkin-Rice House—Garden Front showing close Grouping of Windows

Fig. 70

Larkin-Rice House—Stair Hall Looking towards Front Door

Fig. 71

Larkin-Rice House—Interior view of Drawing Room Window

This window is a beautiful piece of American Regency detail—quite in a modernistic spirit.

HENRY SHERBURNE HOUSE—Circa 1725
Portsmouth

This is a truly fine specimen of a fully developed "Colonial" house of the first quarter of the 1700's. It has great dignity and beauty of proportion. Its doorway carries a splendid example of a Georgian scrolled pediment, similar to that of the Sparhawk House built for Sir William Pepperell's daughter across the Piscataqua at Kittery Point, and also to the door of the great Hill House—built about the same time—which formerly stood at Vaughan and Hanover Streets, Portsmouth. There is a photograph of this house in "Lost Examples of Colonial Architecture" (Helburn N. Y. 1931).

The Sherburne house is said to have been built in 1725 by the Hon. Henry Sherburne, a merchant who resided in the first brick house in Portsmouth which stood at the head of the Portsmouth Pier until 1796. Mr. Sherburne was a Member of the King's Council, Treasurer of the Province, and from 1732-1742 the Chief Justice of the Supreme Court of New Hampshire. His wife was Dorothy, sister of Lt. Gov. Wentworth.

Henry Sherburne's son Henry who was born in 1709, and graduated from Harvard in 1728, resided in this house. In 1754 he was chosen Commissioner of Indian Affairs and interviewed the Six Nations. He married Oct. 22, 1740, Sarah, (daughter of Daniel Warner,) who became the mother of sixteen children who were born and grew up in this house. His daughter Sarah married Judge Woodbury Langdon and one of their sons married Dorothea, daughter of John Jacob Astor.

Fig. 72

Henry Sherburne House—General Exterior View

Fig. 73

Henry Sherburne House—Staircase

This early staircase has the prolonged straight lower step which takes all the balusters which are set on a curve, balusters beyond this step being in a straight line. The balusters are all alike as in the English Georgian Work and not in triplets as later in New England. Also the early newel post is plain turned, of the same pattern as the balusters.

Fig. 74

Henry Sherburne House—Doorway

Fig. 75

Fig. 76

PORTSMOUTH PUBLIC LIBRARY
(1809) "THE ACADEMY"

This building was built by the proprietors of the Portsmouth Academy, incorporated in 1808.

William Harris, the beloved schoolmaster conducted the school for many years. Among his pupils was the writer Thomas Bailey Aldrich.

The interior is designed with a wide gallery around the second story, leaving an open well and surrounding balustrade, giving a graceful and open treatment.

Fig. 77

Above—Portsmouth Public Library

The apparently undocumented belief has always been so strong that the end door, unused as a library door, has for many years been inscribed in old fashioned lettering "Charles Bulfinch, Architect, 1809." From time to time, even today, some young salesman ignoring the date will stop to ask whether he can sell any office material to Mr. Bulfinch.

At Right—Portrait of Charles Bulfinch by Matthew Brown

This picture was painted in London in 1786. Bulfinch sent it to his mother in Boston, writing, "you will find it very rough but that is the modish style of painting introduced by Sir Joshua Reynolds. Mr. Copley indeed paints in another manner. His pictures are finished to the utmost nicety, but then—they are *very dear*."

Fig. 78

WENTWORTH-GARDNER HOUSE—1760
Portsmouth

The Wentworth-Gardner house was erected in 1760 by Madam Mark Hunking Wentworth as a gift to her son Thomas. A perfect Georgian type at the very acme of the Colonial period.

The carving of the house, the greater part in the hall, required a period of fourteen months.

The Key of the window arch is carved as a face, said to be that of the Queen, reigning at the time.

The hall is the great glory of the house.

The period of the house does not call for mantels. The North Parlor has over the fireplace a 48 inch panel of a single piece of pine. The mantel of the South Parlor was probably added in 1790.

The great Kitchen has a windmill in the flue to turn the spit. The fireplace has a trammel and lug-pole used before spits for roasting.

There is a Spinning Attic.

The blocked front of the house was discovered underneath the modern layer of clapboards. The Pineapple over the door, emblem of hospitality, is a restoration. This house was purchased in 1796 by Maj. William Gardner—whose business office was over an "Arch" constructed by him across Gardner St. beside the house. No picture of this "arch" is available or can be traced in any way. The house is owned by the Metropolitan Museum of New York—but is in charge of the Society for the Preservation of New England Antiquities.

Fig. 79

WENTWORTH-GARDNER HOUSE—GENERAL EXTERIOR VIEW FROM STREET

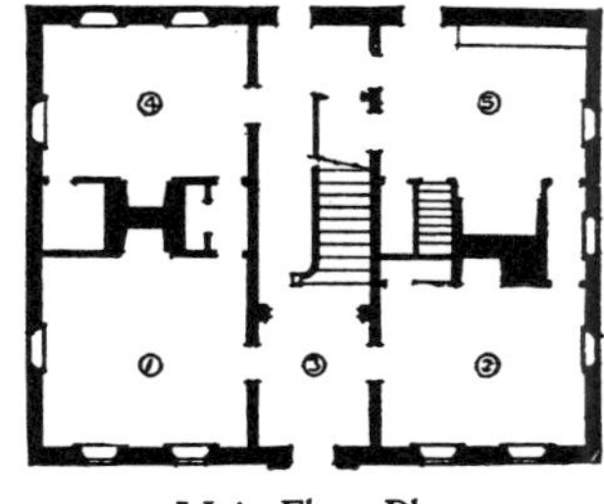

Main Floor Plan

Fig. 80

Fig. 81

WENTWORTH-GARDNER HOUSE—WOODEN PINEAPPLE OVER FRONT DOOR

This pineapple, with green leaves and gilded apple, replaced an earlier ornament after the blocking was discovered underneath the clapboarded front of the house.

Fig. 82

WENTWORTH-GARDNER HOUSE—ENTRANCE DOOR

For many years the wood blocking was hidden and forgotten under later clapboards.

Courtesy Metropolitan Museum of Art

Fig. 83

WENTWORTH-GARDNER HOUSE—STAIRWAY

The newel post is in one piece, the spiral being carved from the outside by the remarkable ship carvers who were common in the old days in the maritime towns of New England. The hand rail, as in all houses of this period, is painted pine; mahogany not coming in for this purpose, strangely enough, until taste began to decline. The spindles, in sets of three, are in old black cherry.

Courtesy Metropolitan Museum of Art

Fig. 84

WENTWORTH-GARDNER HOUSE—DINING ROOM

The furniture of the period is loaned by Portsmouth residents.

Fig. 85

WENTWORTH-GARDNER HOUSE—LOWER RUN OF STAIR

Fig. 86

WENTWORTH-GARDNER HOUSE—UPPER RUN OF STAIR

Fig. 87

WENTWORTH-GARDNER HOUSE—SECOND STORY HALL

All the walls are treated with a full order of fluted Ionic Pilasters.

Fig. 88

WENTWORTH-GARDNER HOUSE—NORTH DRAWING ROOM

The tile is original. There is no mantel shelf. The upper panel is of one piece of pine 48 inches wide.

Fig. 89

WENTWORTH-GARDNER HOUSE—DINING ROOM

The fire-place has no mantel, only mouldings.

Fig. 90

WENTWORTH-GARDNER HOUSE—A BEDROOM

The panelling runs from floor to ceiling.

Fig. 91

WENTWORTH-GARDNER HOUSE—SOUTH DRAWING ROOM

Fig. 92

WENTWORTH-GARDNER HOUSE—UPSTAIRS BED ROOM

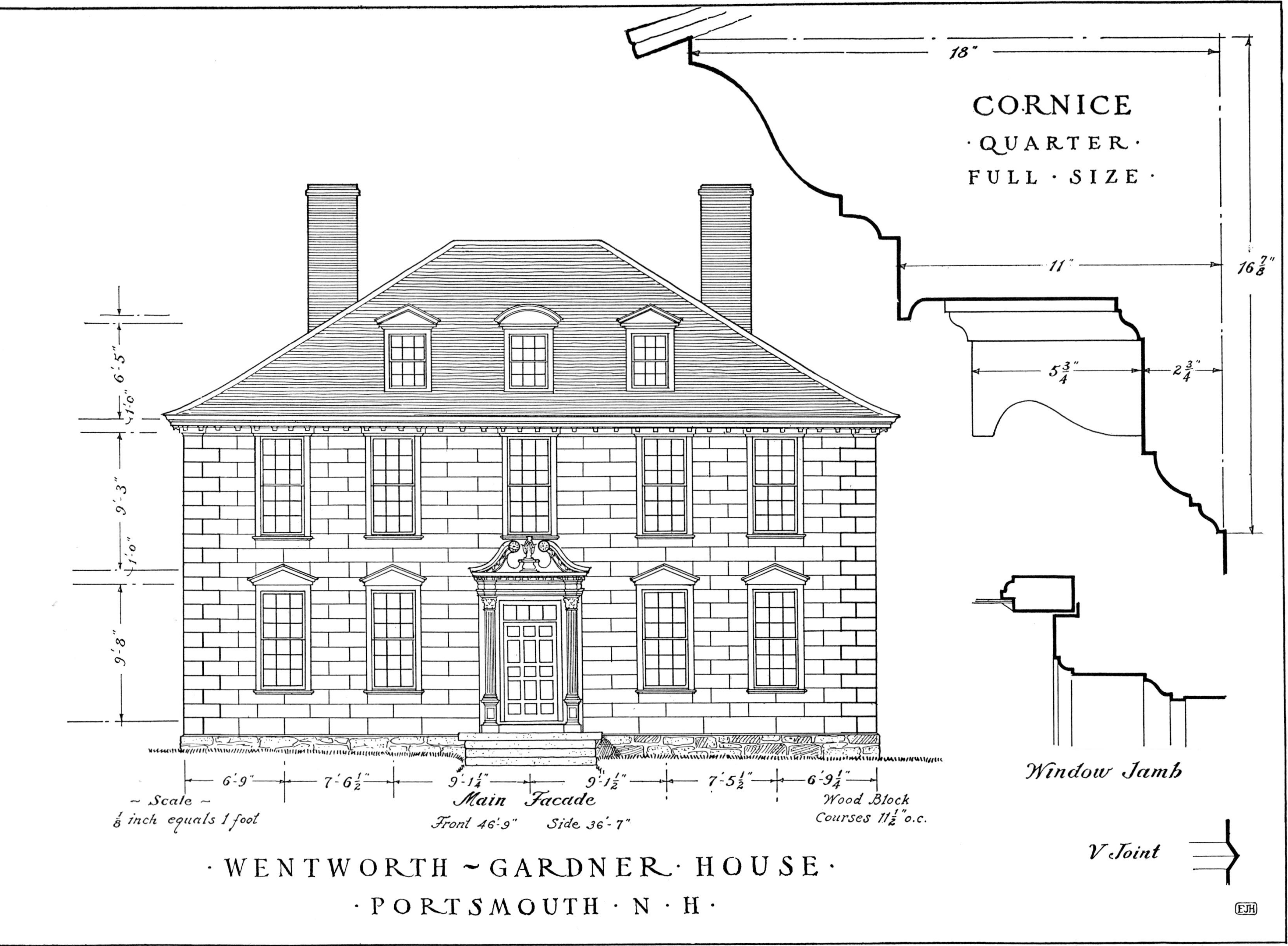

Courtesy of Edwin J. Hipkiss, Esq., and the Architectural Forum

Fig. 93

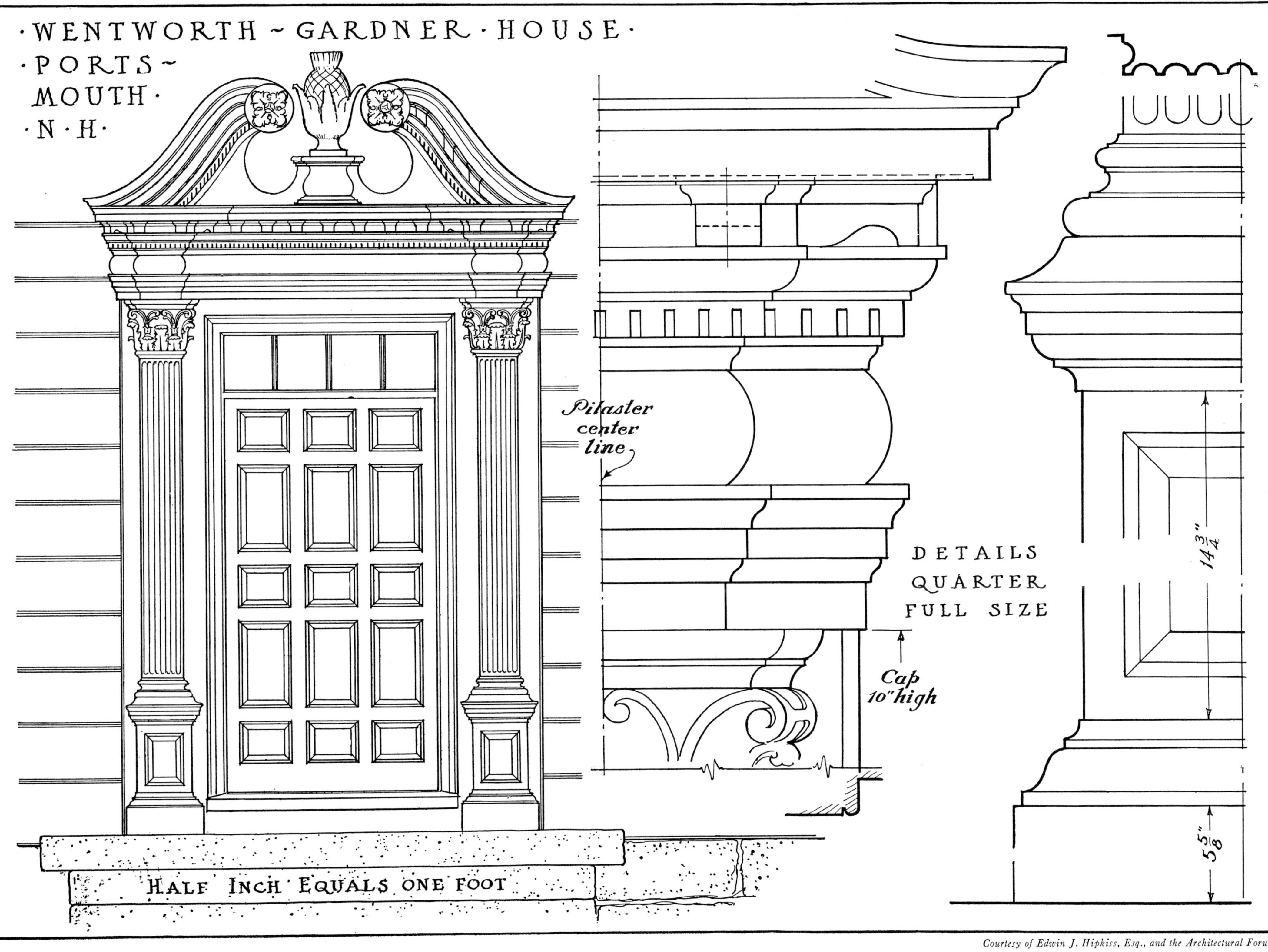

Courtesy of Edwin J. Hipkiss, Esq., and the Architectural Forum

Fig. 94

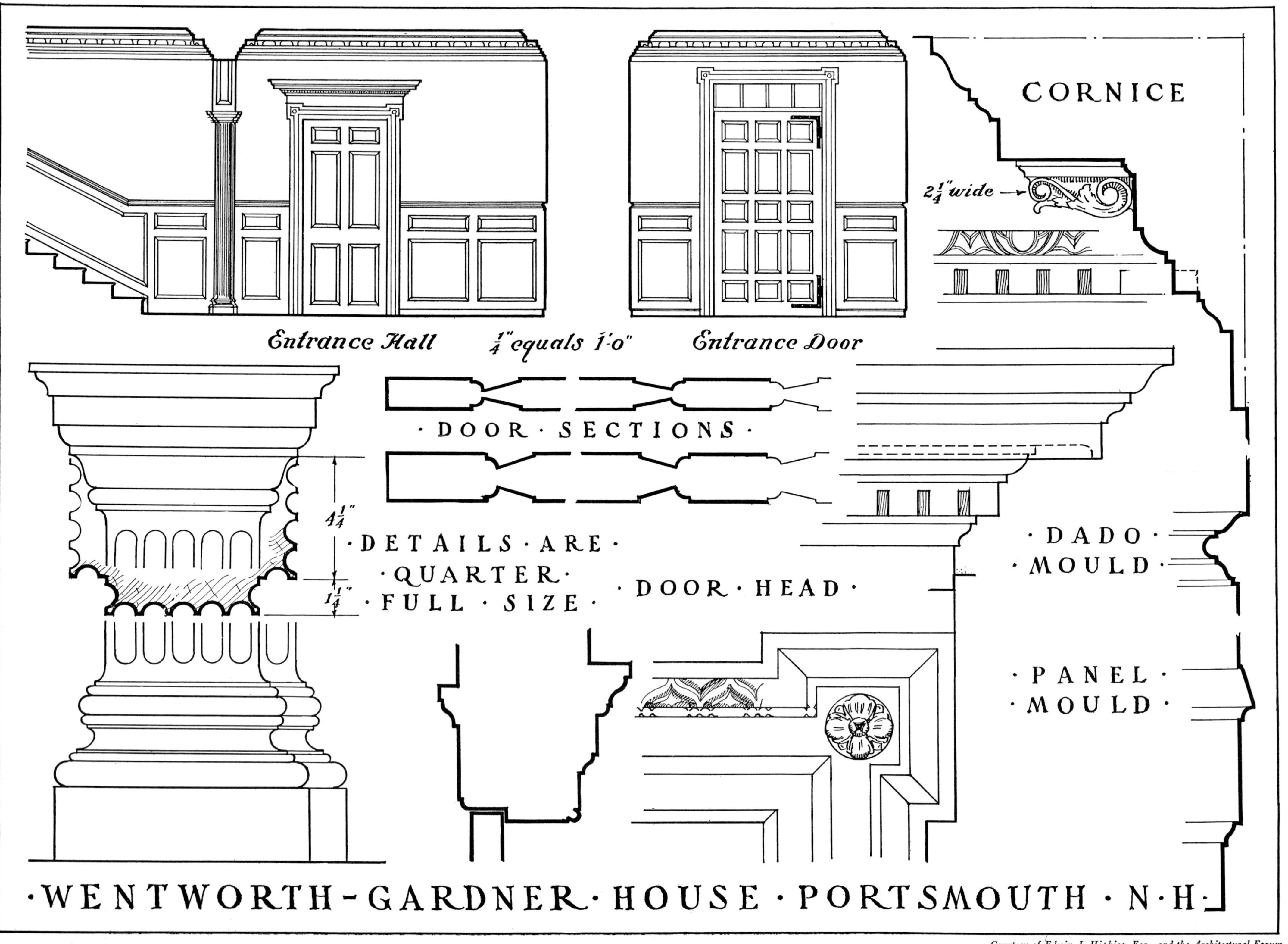

Courtesy of Edwin J. Hipkiss, Esq., and the Architectural Forum

Fig. 95

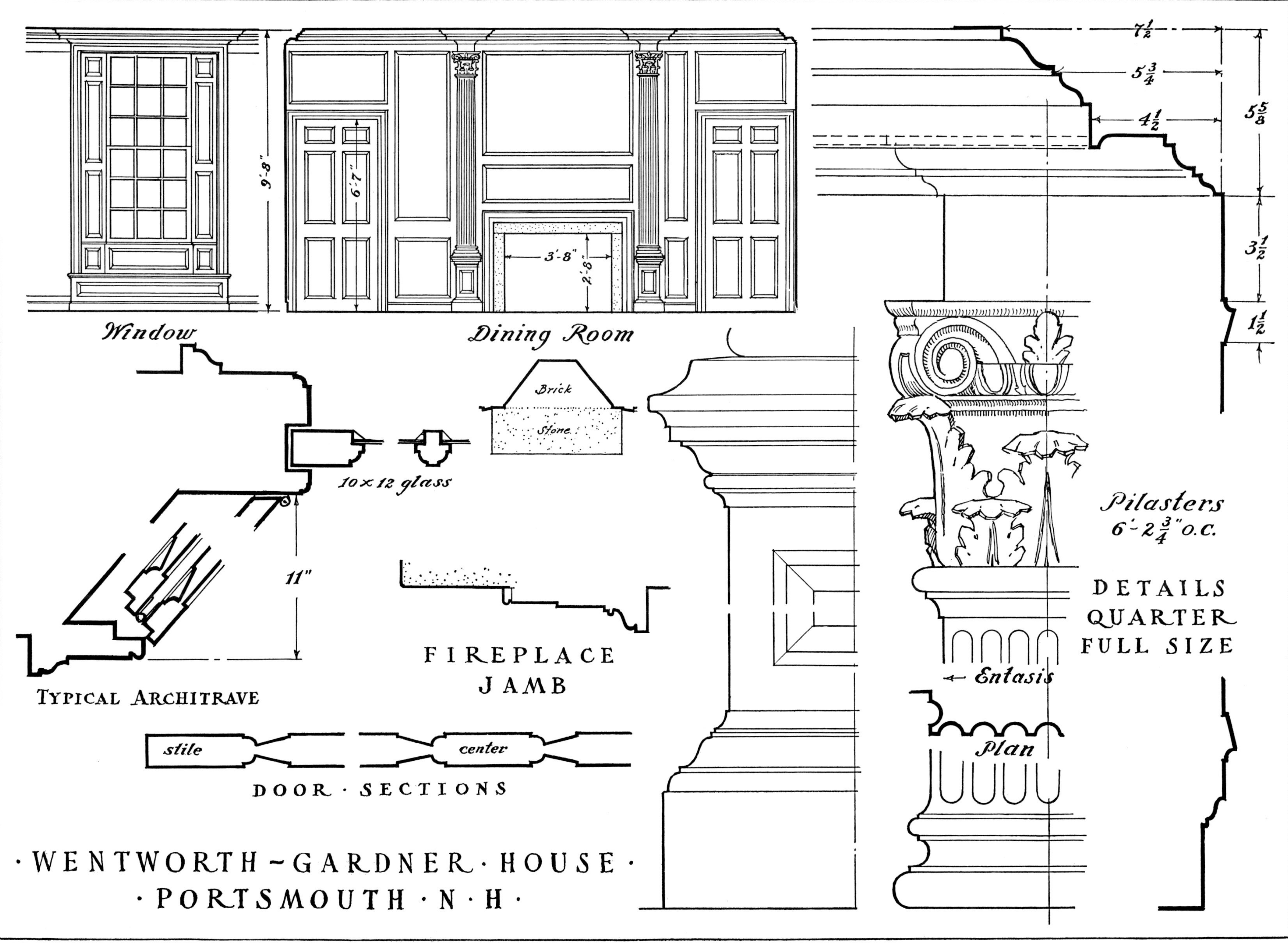

Fig. 96

Courtesy of Edwin J. Hipkiss, Esq., and the Architectural Forum

JEWETT MEMORIAL (Sarah Orne Jewett House) 1774
South Berwick, Maine

The stair and woodwork of the upper and lower halls took two men one hundred days to complete. This shows that such work was done by skilled experts, otherwise more than two men would have been employed.

From 1774 to 1838, the wainscoting was never painted, by which time the wood was a rich dark brown, "the color of mahogany." This is interesting as proving once more that the universal habit of painting "Colonial" interior woodwork white was not a Colonial habit at all. The "Colonial" builders left their woodwork unpainted, or painted it in gayer and warmer tones.

In this house, Sarah Orne Jewett, the writer, was born and spent most of her life. It was bequeathed by Miss Mary Jewett to her nephew, Dr. Theodore Eastman, and by him left to the Society for the Preservation of New England Antiquities. It was built in 1774 by John Higgins. The wall paper in one of the front chambers was originally intended for the Governor of one of the French West Indies, but was taken from a vessel captured by an American privateer. It was brought into Salem and bought by Captain Jewett.

Fig. 97

SARAH ORNE JEWETT HOUSE—FRONT ENTRANCE

Fig. 98

Fig. 99

Sarah Orne Jewett House—Two exteriors from the curving Portland Road

Fig. 100

Fig. 101

Sarah Orne Jewett House—Great Hall looking in two Directions

Fig. 102

Sarah Orne Jewett House—Upstairs room with canopied bed

Fig. 103

Sarah Orne Jewett House—Upper Stairs and Stair Hall

Fig. 104

Sarah Orne Jewett House—Dining Room showing tall clock

Fig. 105

Sarah Orne Jewett House—Dining Room showing Muskets and Powder Horns

CUTTER-LANGDON MANSION—Circa 1750
Portsmouth

This house was built about 1750 for Jacob Treadwell by his parents, Mr. and Mrs. Charles Treadwell. It was probably built by George Gains, a cabinet-maker and house carpenter, whose father, George Gains, Sr. had built Mr. Charles Treadwell's house on Congress Street (long since demolished). The present unfortunate front door is an addition of the eighties. The Treadwells built fine houses for all their children. For their daughter Hannah, who married Dr. Ammi R. Cutter, they built a house on the corner of Congress and Fleet Streets (where the offices of the New Hampshire Gas and Electric Company are now situated). On the corner of State and Fleet Streets they built the house now occupied by the Y. W. C. A. for their son Nathaniel. And on the corner of Congress and Middle Streets they built this fine house for Jacob.

Some of the Treadwell fortune was lost in the burning of Moscow.

This house was purchased some years later by Dr. Ammi R. Cutter.

In 1817 President James Monroe and his suite visited here.

It is to be regretted that the position of this splendid house, directly on the busy corner of a through route for motor traffic, is a danger to its being preserved indefinitely.

Fig. 106

Cutter-Langdon Mansion—Exterior

Fig. 107

Cutter-Langdon Mansion—Front Drawing Room

The Front Drawing Room is a fine example of the early heavy true Colonial Georgian work. The great weight of the wood cornice, and its curved frieze are of the true English type. The mantelpiece itself may have been, and probably was, added later, as the date of 1750 did not call for mantel shelves. It is, however, well in character.

Fig. 108

CUTTER-LANGDON MANSION—ENTRANCE HALL SHOWING SPLENDID ARCH AND STAIR.

Fig. 109

CUTTER-LANGDON MANSION—STAIR WINDOW

This fine window came from the George Haven house, when it was taken down in 1904 to make room for the senior high school, just west of the Public Library—a most regrettable exchange architecturally.

GOVERNOR BENNING WENTWORTH MANSION
1695 and 1750
Little Harbor, N. H.

This house was owned by Benning Wentworth, appointed Royal Governor of New Hampshire at the time of the final separation of this state from Massachusetts in 1741.

There is evidence that he inherited the house from his grandfather, who built it about 1695. The Governor added to it the more imposing series of rooms in 1750.

The great house at Little Harbor, two miles from the centre of Portsmouth town, now contains twenty-four original living rooms, and had a larger number in earlier days. Its colonial features remain otherwise unchanged. Tradition has it that the ample series of cellars stabled a troop of thirty horses for defense in time of danger.

The original entrance door (which contains an old wooden lock of mammoth size) opens into a small entrance hall flanked by wall bench seats, over which a line of large wooden pegs served to hold visitor's cloaks; and above them, in double sets, hang ten flint lock muskets with fixed bayonets, marked in French "Manufactury of the King at Ste. Etienne, 1759." Possibly these muskets came from the capture of Louisburg, which expedition Wentworth asked to command.

Through this hall one enters the Council Chamber where the councillors were summoned in these words: "Governor Wentworth's compliments, and commands you to come to Little Harbor to drink the King's health."

It was in this same Council Chamber that the widowed Governor, at a dinner party, announced his intention to marry the lively young Patty Hilton, daughter of Judge Hilton of Portsmouth, which ceremony the Reverend Arthur Brown proceeded to perform. This incident gave Longfellow his theme for the "Ballad of Lady Wentworth," in the "Tales of a Wayside Inn."

Photograph by Lieut. John Prescott

Fig. 110

Governor Benning Wentworth Mansion—General View from the Water

Fig. 111

Governor Benning Wentworth Mansion—Dining Room

Fig. 112

Governor Benning Wentworth Mansion—Parlor

The original block paper on the walls was from England or France about 1750.

Fig. 113

Governor Benning Wentworth Mansion—Council Chamber

Fig. 114

Governor Benning Wentworth Mansion—Exterior

Fig. 115

Fig. 116

Captain Samuel Chauncey House (1808) 218 Islington Street, Portsmouth
(sometimes called Captain Barnes House)

This fine old type of the three story town house was demolished in 1936 by an oil company to make way for a filling station. Here is shown the front on Islington Street, and the coach-house in the rear.

Fig. 117

Captain Samuel Chauncey House

At an early age Samuel Chauncey went to sea; becoming a supercargo and later a Master of ships owned by Col. Eliphalet Ladd, a wealthy shipowner and merchant. In later years Capt. Chauncey became a business partner, and in 1795 he married the Colonel's daughter Betsy. In 1807 Captain Chauncey purchased the property on Islington Street where he erected the commodious dwelling and out buildings, and here the Chauncey family resided until 1815 when the Captain became uneasy and felt that he would like to go to sea again. He sailed from Portsmouth as commander of the Hannah, bound for Bremen. This was his last command for news soon reached Portsmouth that Captain Chauncey had ended his life by suicide.

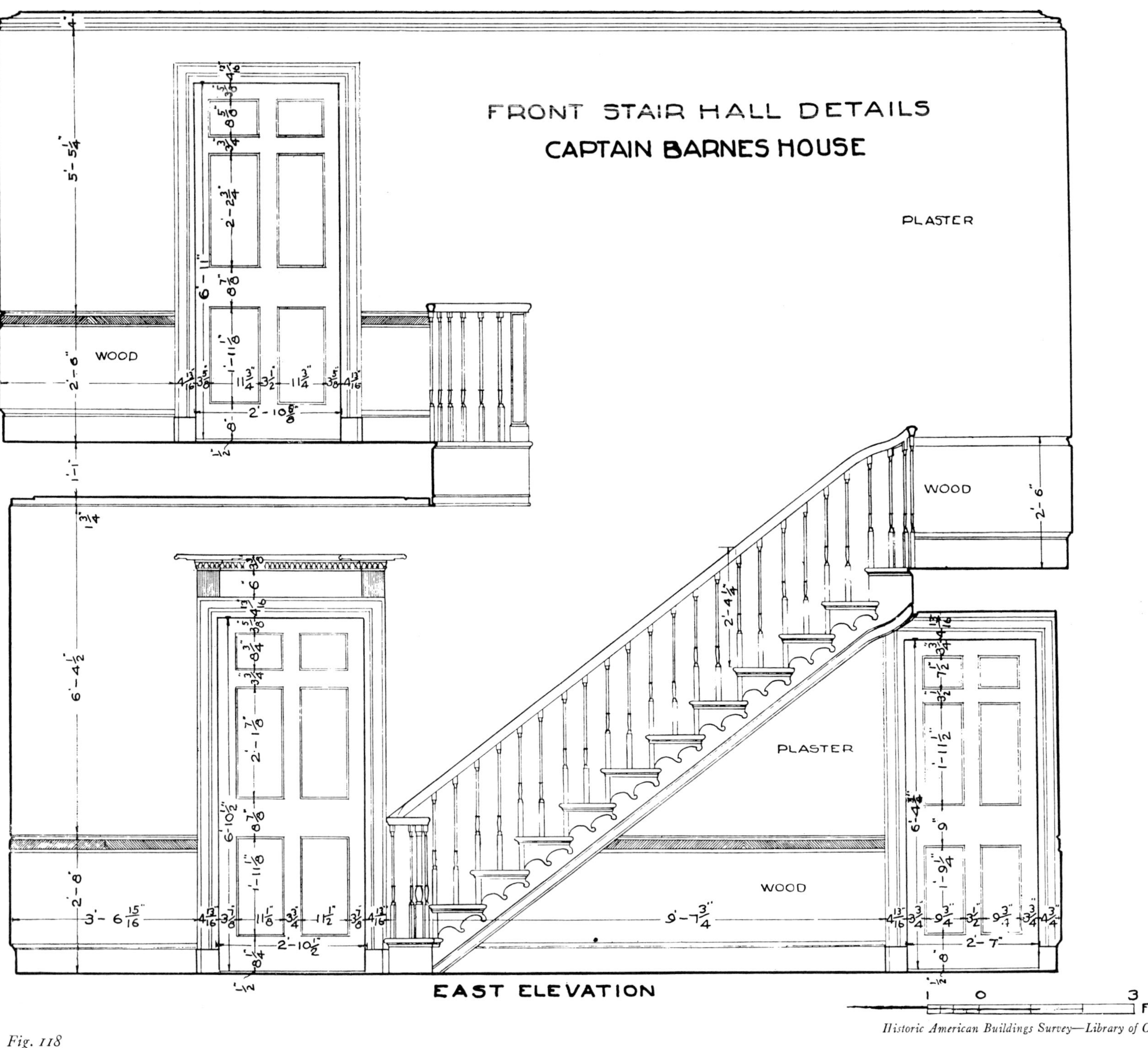

Historic American Buildings Survey—Library of Congress

Fig. 118

CEILING LINE
PLASTER LINE
SECTION A-A
PLASTER LINE
4 1/8"
LINE OF DADO
SECTION B-B
SECTION C-C
CAPTAIN BARNES HOUSE
FRONT STAIR HALL DETAILS
1
0
3
INCHES

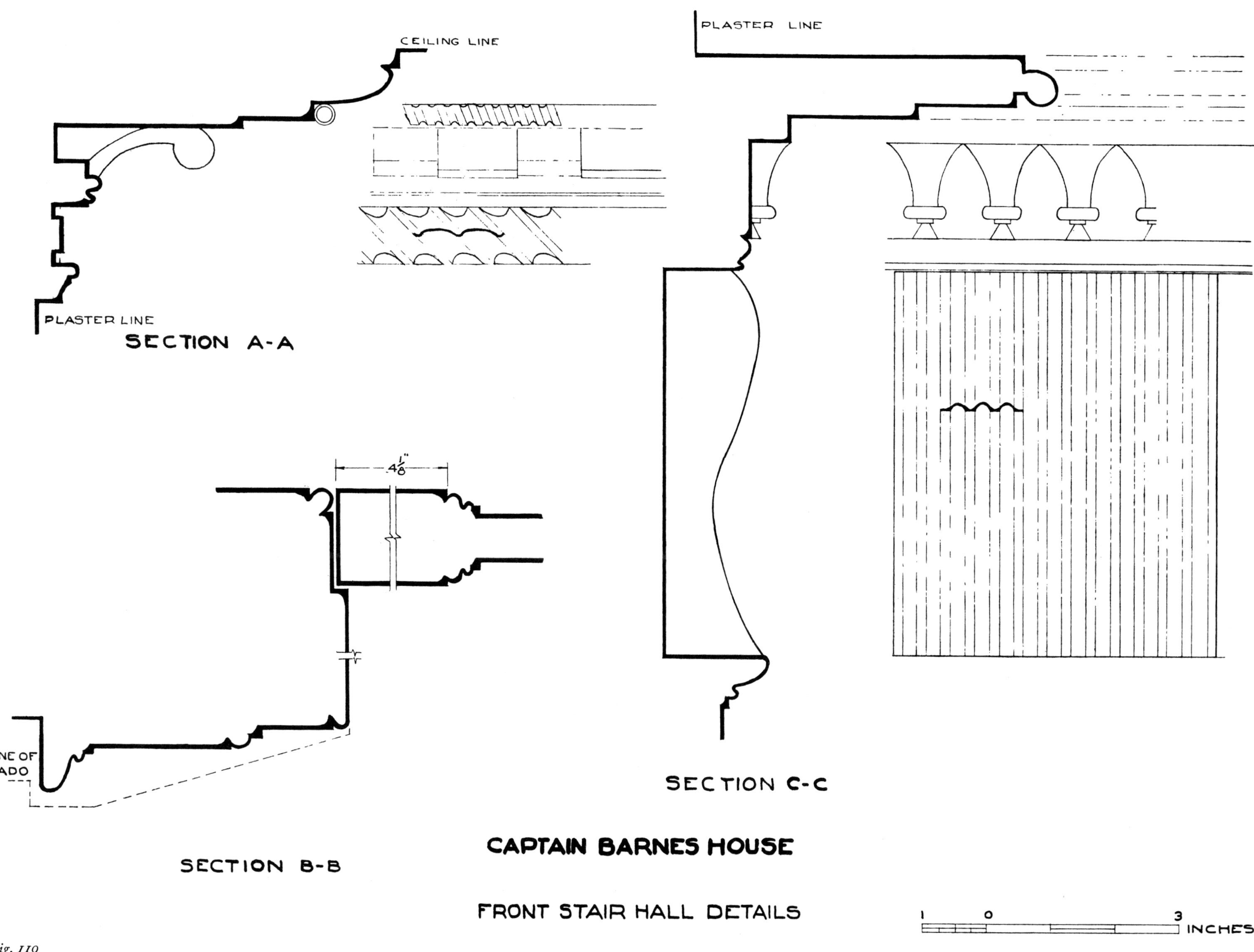

Fig. 119

Fig. 120

CAPTAIN SAMUEL CHAUNCEY HOUSE—MANTELPIECE

This mantel of painted pine and various varnished hardwoods, together with the cornice and wainscot here shown—also the staircase and other mantels—has been rescued and admirably set up in the remodelled house of Mr. and Mrs. Storer Decatur at Kittery Point, Maine. The restoration was completed in 1937.

PLASTER
PLASTER
MARBLE
WOOD
PLAST-ER
PLAST-ER
SIDE
SOUTH ELEVATION
SOFFIT
NOTE - DOTTED LINE INDICATES CORNICE
PLAN ABOVE MANTEL
NEW DOOR OPENING
D-112
MARBLE HEARTH
CAPTAIN BARNES HOUSE
SITTING ROOM
FEET

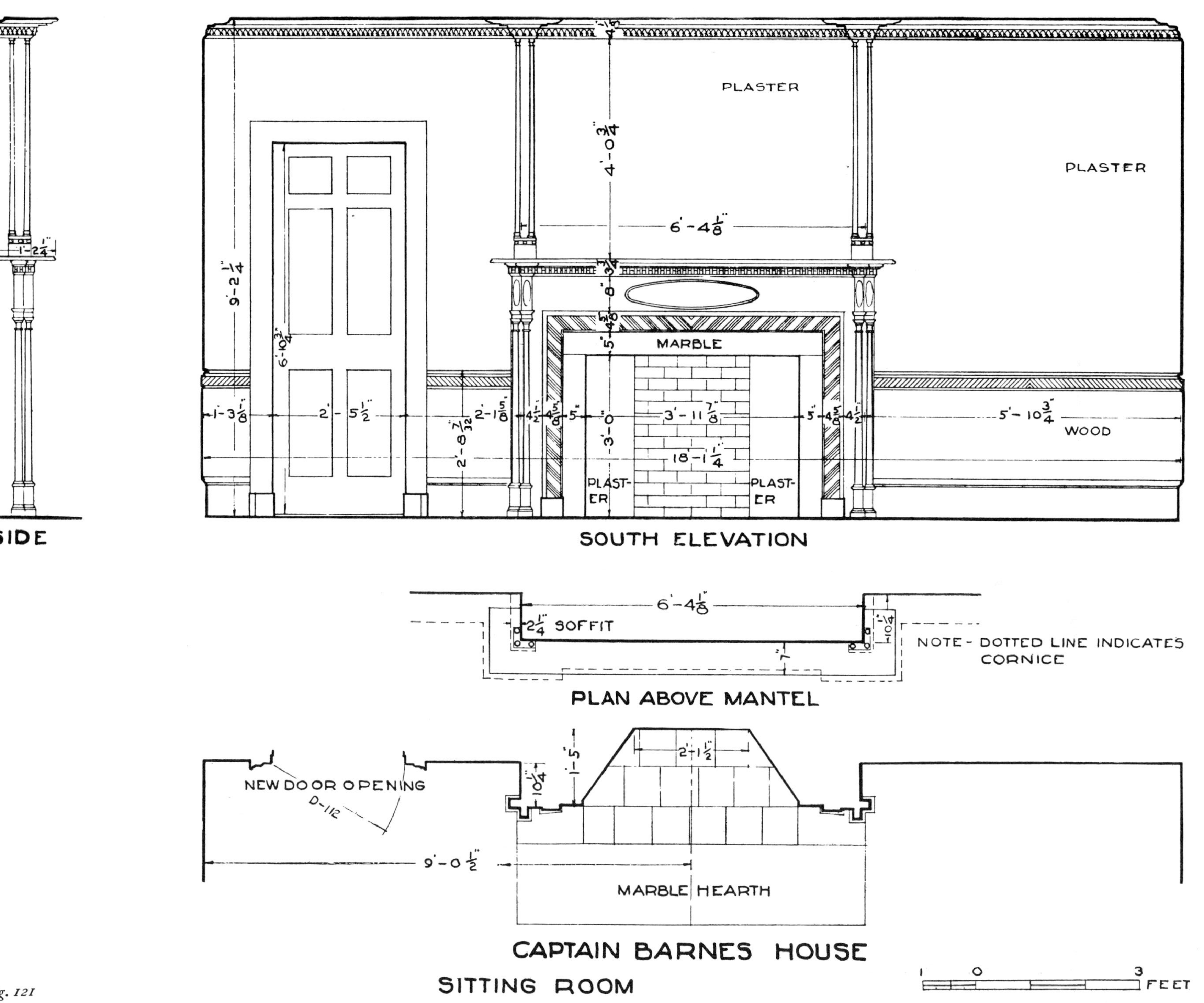

Fig. 121

CAPTAIN BARNES HOUSE
MARBLE
8"
5"
SECTION THROUGH MANTEL
EBONY
MEDIUM COLOR
LIGHT COLOR
ALTERNATING EBONY & LIGHT COLOR
LIGHT COLOR
DETAIL OF INLAY "B"
LIGHT COLOR
EBONY
DARK COLOR
ALTERNATING EBONY & LIGHT COLOR
DETAIL OF INLAY "A"
MEDIUM COLOR
ALTERNATING EBONY & LIGHT COLOR
EBONY
LIGHT COLOR
DARK COLOR
DETAIL OF INLAY "A"
DARK COLOR
SEE ENLARGED DETAIL
MEDIUM COLOR
EBONY
DETAIL OF INLAY "B"
SITTING ROOM DETAILS
1 0 3 INCHES
1 0 6 INCHES

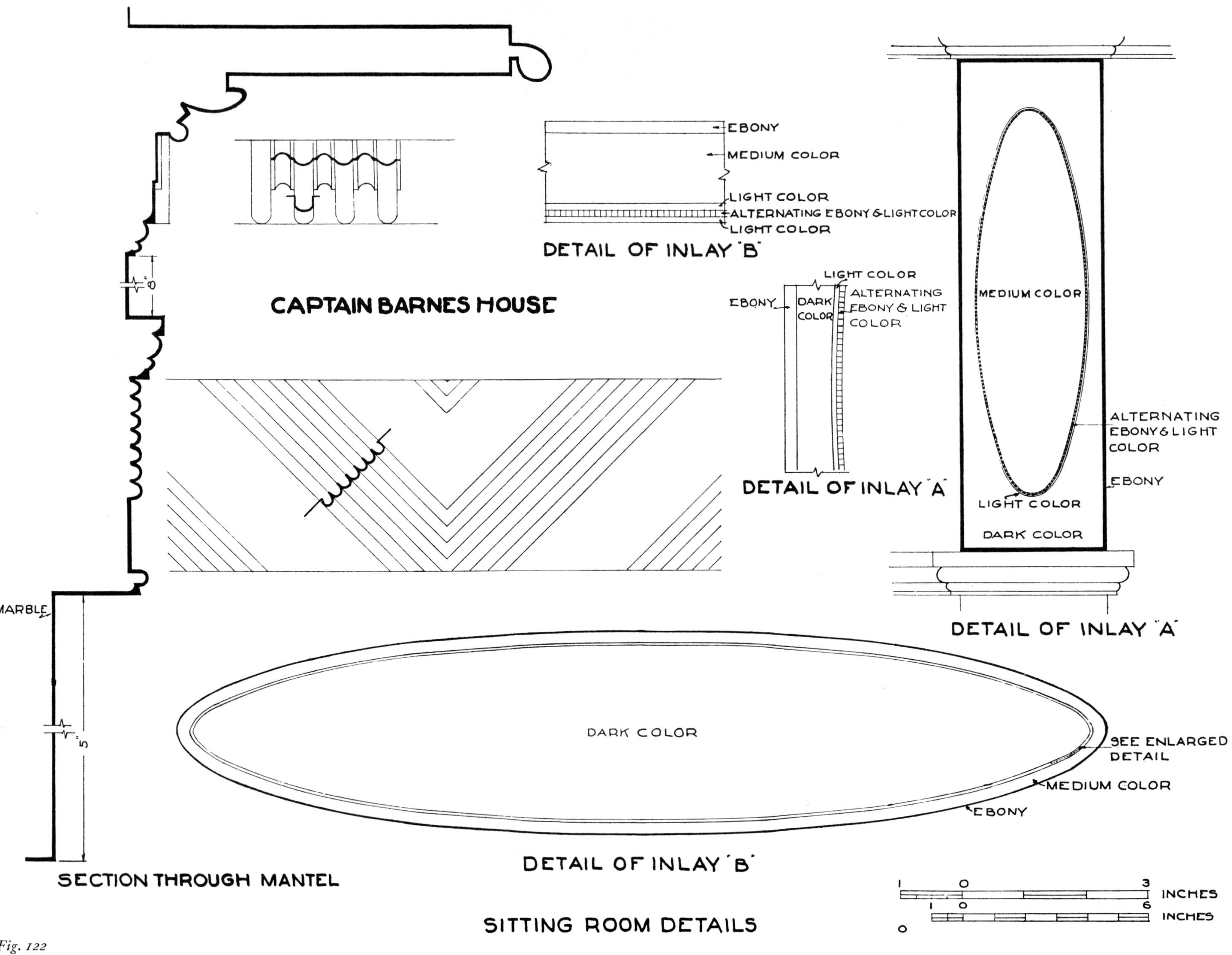

Fig. 122

SITTING ROOM DETAILS
PLASTER LINE
NOTE - DIMENSIONS ON COLUMN SHAFTS ARE TAKEN AT 1" INTERVALS BEGINNING AT TOP OF SHAFT.
WOOD - ON SAME LINE AS PLASTER
PLAN OF COLUMN
WOOD
PLASTER LINE
CORNICE
SQUARE
TURNED
SQUARE
2'-9½"
TURNED
3'-5⅝"
PLASTER LINE
OPEN
OPEN
PLASTER LINE
CAPTAIN BARNES HOUSE
FLOOR
MANTEL
INCHES
ELEVATION OF COLUMN BELOW MANTEL
ELEVATION OF COLUMN ABOVE MANTEL

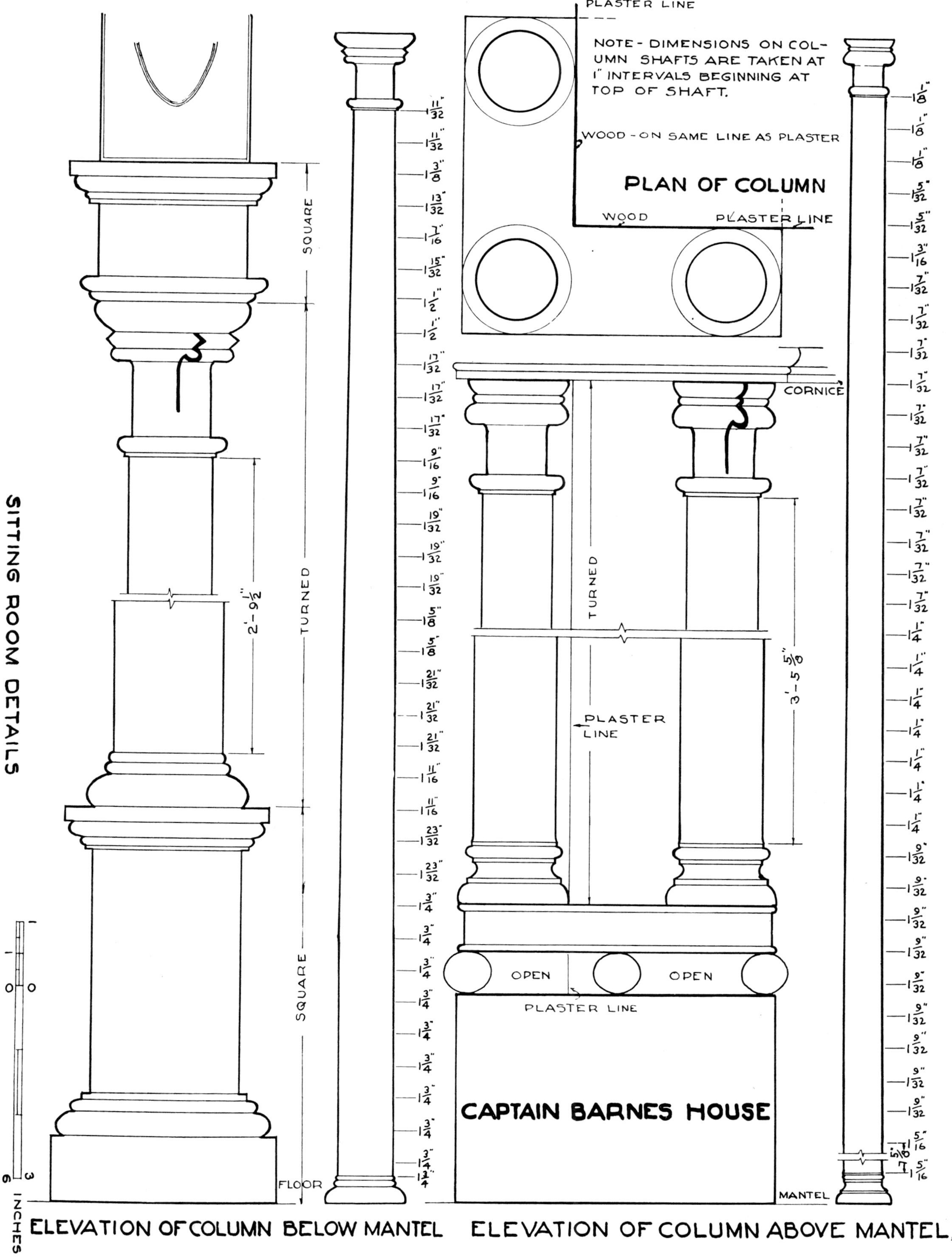

Fig. 123

Fig. 124

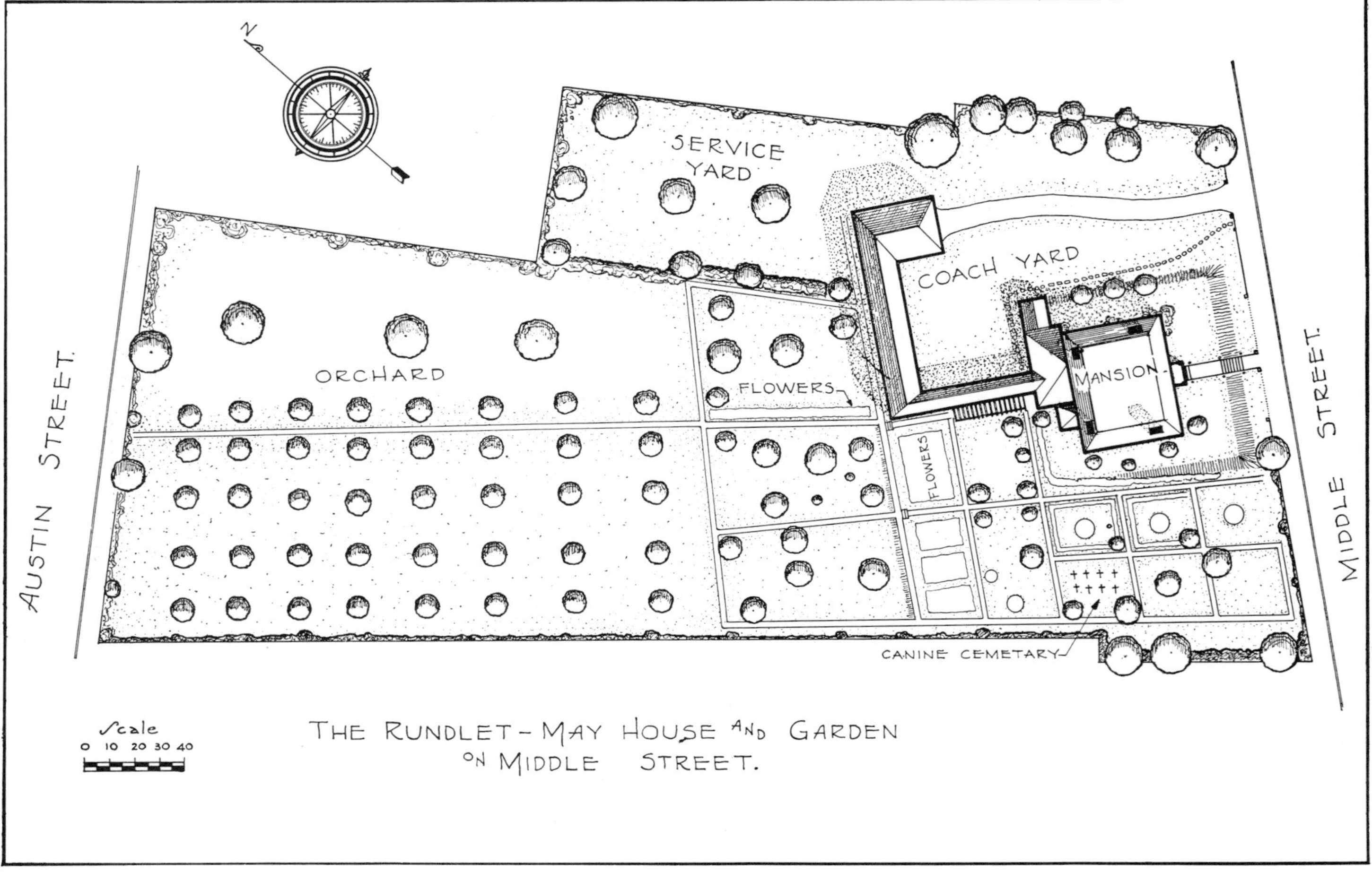

Fig. 125

RUNDLET-MAY HOUSE—COACH-HOUSE AND STABLE YARD

A very interesting example of a stable yard to a town house. The two rows of arches were evidently not of the same epoch, but the final effect is good.

Fig. 126

RUNDLET-MAY HOUSE (1806-7) 364 MIDDLE STREET, PORTSMOUTH

This house was built by James Rundlet, a merchant whose Counting House was on Market Street. Mr. Rundlet had a family of thirteen children and so this spacious dwelling was none too large to house his growing family. It is said that when he built the house he could stand in his front door and, as far as the eye could reach, to the south and to the west, all the wooded countryside was his. The hill over which Highland Street now passes was called "Rundlet's Mountain."

James Rundlet's daughter Louisa married Mr. George May whose descendants still occupy the house.

This is a truly fine and dignified type of the early 19th Century mansion, and its position, back from and above the street, adds to its impressiveness.

Fig. 127

RUNDLET-MAY HOUSE—DRAWING ROOM MANTEL

Fig. 128

RUNDLET-MAY HOUSE—WINDOW ON STAIR LANDING

Note the fluted pilasters without definite caps and the quarter round colonettes in the casing. Also the vertical line of the pedestal behind the chair backs.

Fig. 129

Livermore House (1735) 32 Livermore Street, Portsmouth—Entrance Motif

Fig. 130

Livermore House

This white gambrel roofed house formerly stood in Haven Park on the S. E. corner facing Pleasant Street. It was swung around to its present location in 1900 when the Park was cleared.

Fig. 131

Buckminster House (1720) 1 Islington Street, Portsmouth

Daniel Warner, who came here from Ipswich, Mass., built this house. It was the birthplace of his son, the Hon. Jonathan Warner who married Mary Macpheadris.

Fig. 132

Levi Woodbury House—Detail of wall paper in N. E. Bedroom, 2nd floor

Fig. 133

Detail in present Dining Room

Fig. 134

Stairway

Fig. 135

Levi Woodbury House—View from Grounds

Fig. 136

Living Room Mantel

Fig. 137

Detail showing painted work with hard wood panels

Fig. 138

GOV. LEVI WOODBURY HOUSE (1809) CHRISTIAN SHORE, PORTSMOUTH

This house was built by Captain Samuel Ham.

Gurney writes: "When the house was completed, he celebrated the event by giving quite an elaborate reception to his friends and neighbors. At its conclusion, and after his guests had all departed, he went into one of the upper chambers, and for some reason unknown, committed suicide by hanging."

In 1819 the Hon. Levi Woodbury came to Portsmouth and purchased the estate. He was at one time a presidential probability.

GOV. LEVI WOODBURY MANSION
SECTION OF CORNICE
CEILING
SECTION AT E-E
WALL LINE
PLASTER
ELEVATION OF CORNICE
ELEVATION OF DADO CAP
PLASTER
WINDOW & DOOR TRIM BASE
SHUTTER 5'-9" X 3'-0½"
SEE SHEET 16 FOR DETAIL
PLASTER
SASH
DOOR
SECTION OF DADO
SECTION OF A-A
ELEVATION OF SIDE WINDOW
ELEVATION OF DOOR NO.120
DETAILS OF DINING ROOM
FEET
INCHES
METRIC

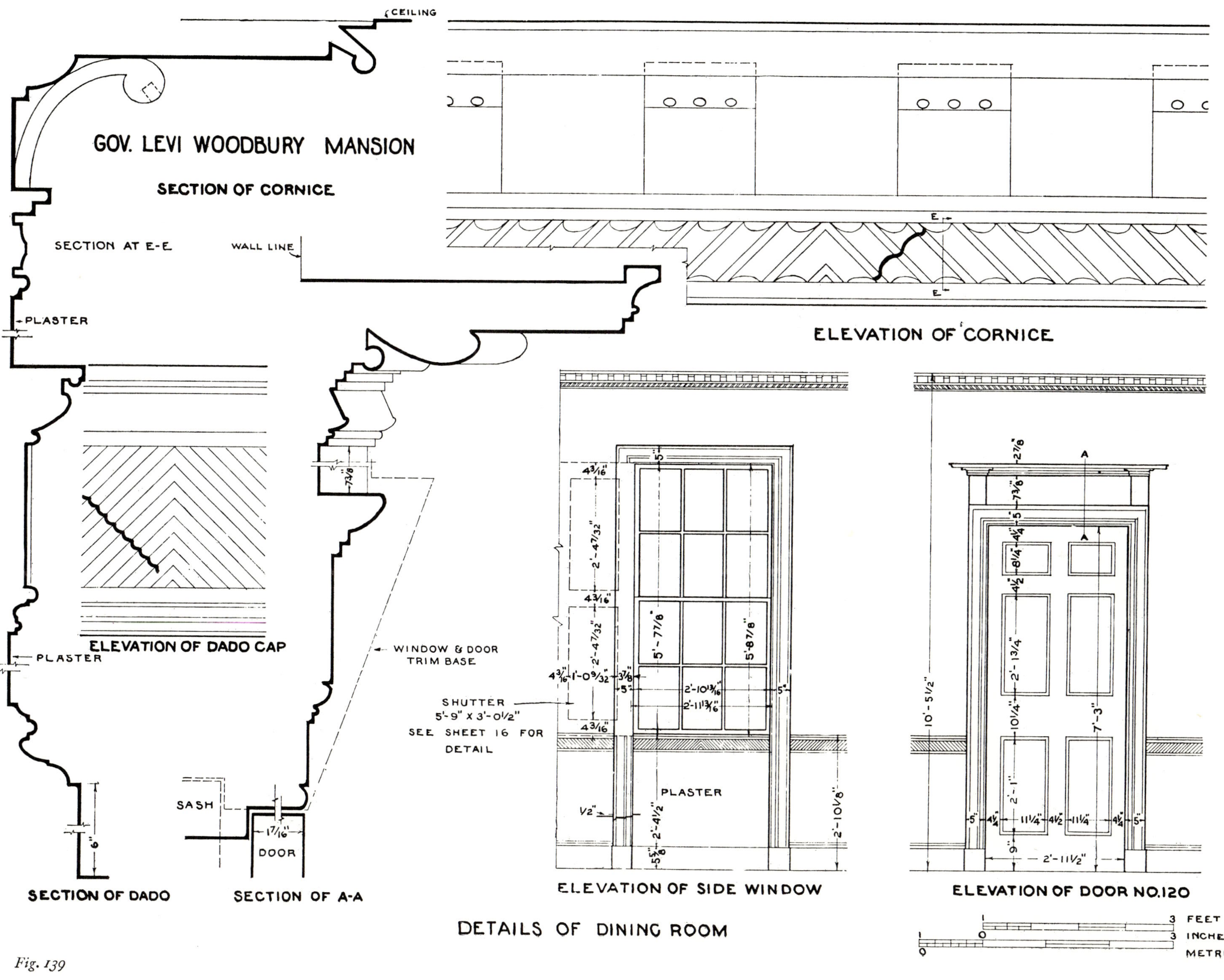

Fig. 139

DADO CAP PARALLEL WITH HAND RAIL
SECTION OF DADO
MAHOGANY
BIRDSEYE MAPLE VENEER
MAHOGANY
SECTION OF HAND RAIL
ELEVATION OF BALUSTER
PLAN
SECTION OF STAIR NOSING
2' - 11 5/16"
ELEVATION OF NEWEL POST
SCROLL ON STAIR ABOVE LANDING
SCROLL ON STAIR BELOW LANDING
GOV. LEVI WOODBURY MANSION
TYPICAL SCROLL ON STAIR END
PLASTER
DETAILS OF STAIRS
1
0
3 INCHES

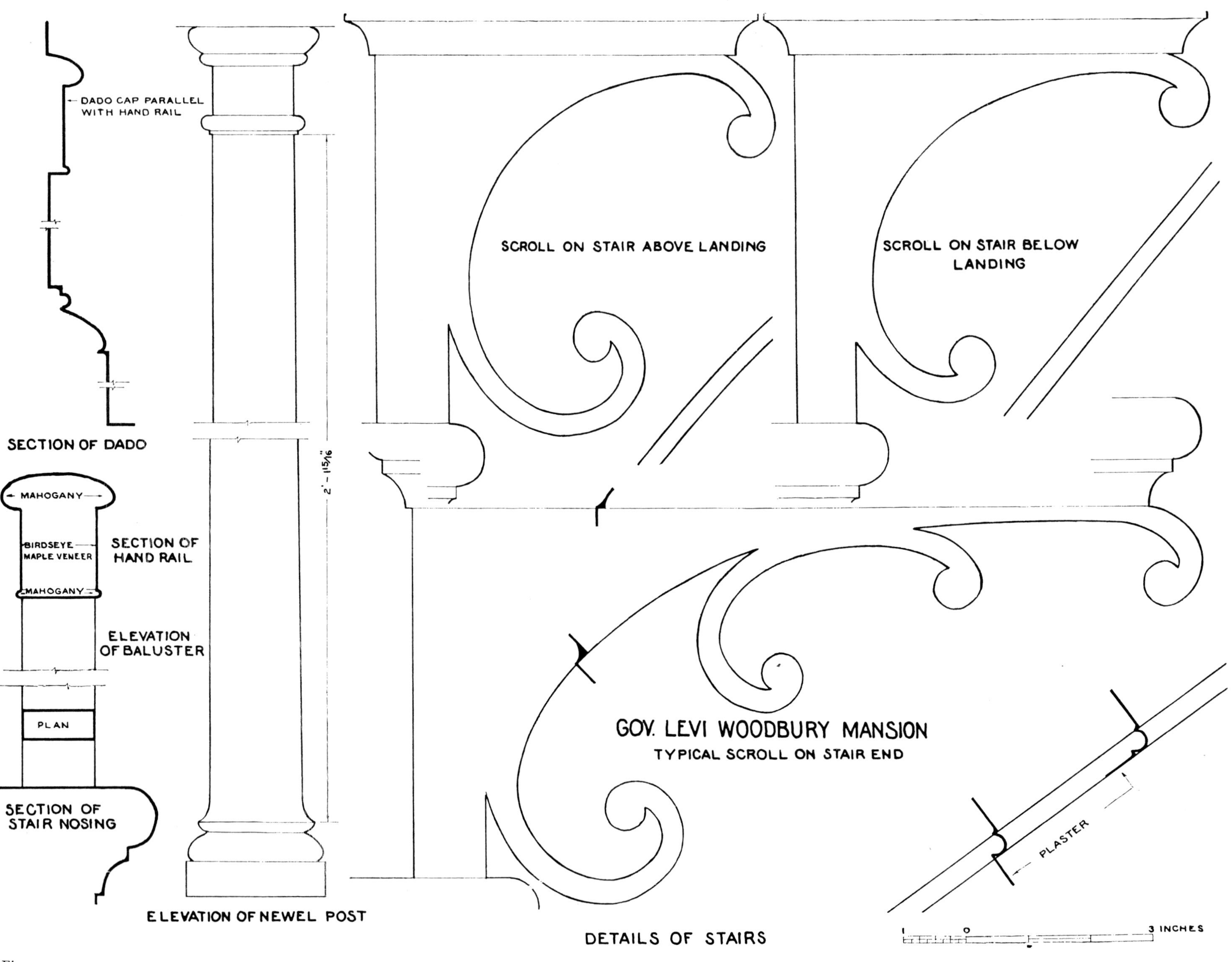

Fig. 140

CEILING
CORNICE IN 2ND FL. STAIRHALL
PLASTER
DADO IN 1ST FL. STAIRHALL
CORNICE IN 3RD FL. STAIRHALL
WOOD PANEL
1'-9 3/16"
BASEBOARD IN 2ND & 3RD FL. STAIRHALLS
4 1/2"
7 11/16"
DIMENSION 3RD FL.
DIMENSION 2ND FL.
FLOOR
DOOR TRIM IN VESTIBULE
SEE SHEET 34
1 7/8"
PLINTH BLOCK
6 1/2" HIGH
LINE OF RISER
PLAN OF VOLUTE AT 1ST FLOOR STAIR
GOV. LEVI WOODBURY MANSION
0
3 INCHES
STAIRHALL DETAILS

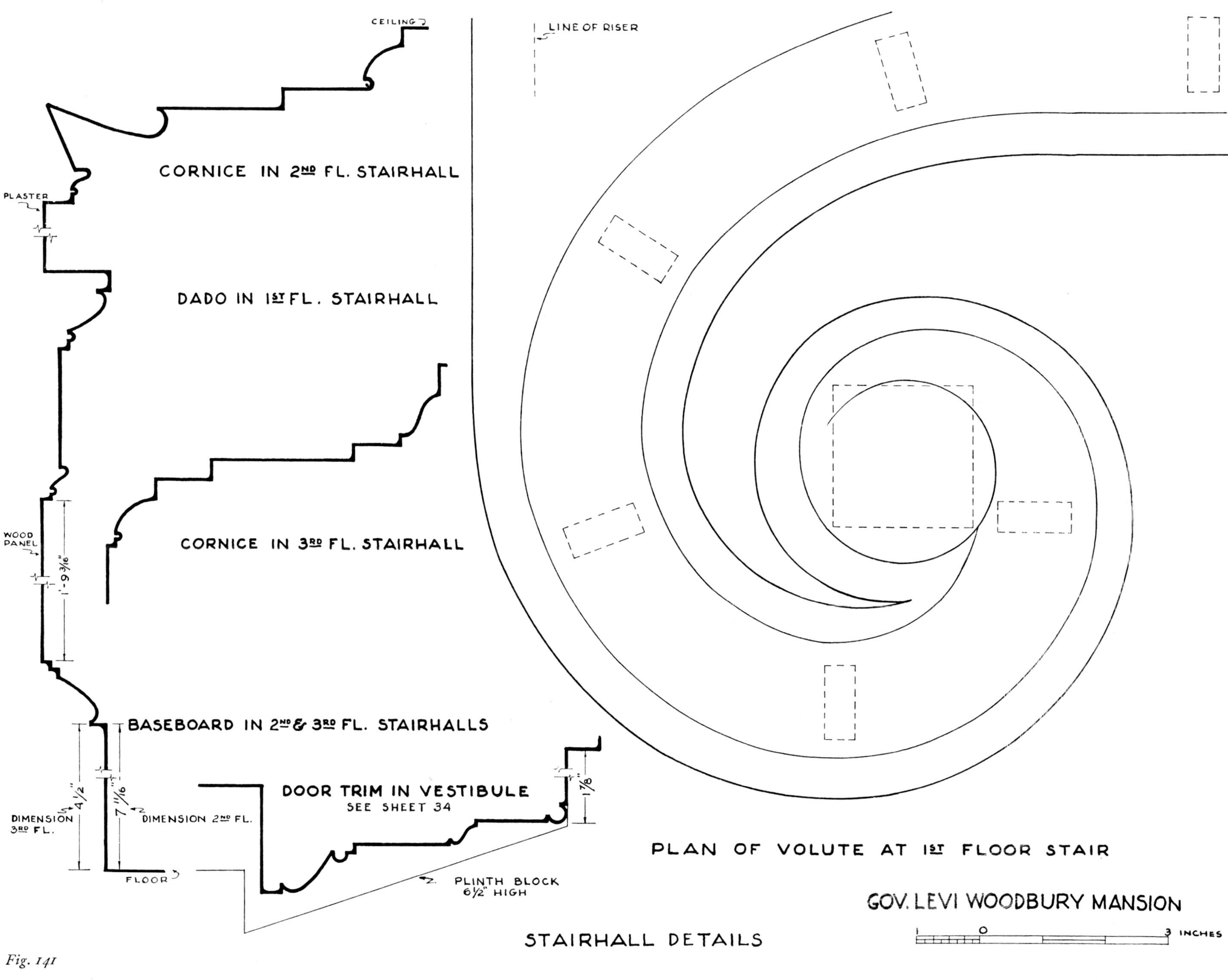

Fig. 141

Fig. 142

Rev. Samuel Langdon House (1749) 134 Pleasant Street, Portsmouth
Entrance and Gate Posts

Fig. 143

REV. SAMUEL LANGDON HOUSE

Rev. Samuel Langdon was a graduate of Harvard, Class of 1740, and soon after came to Portsmouth to teach Latin and mathematics. In 1745 he was Captain of the New Hampshire Regiment at Louisburg, under the command of William Pepperrell. He was pastor of the North Church and resigned to become President of Harvard College.

Fig. 144

TOSCAN'S BUNGALOW (1800) GREENLAND, N. H.

This house was built by Jean Joseph Marie Toscan, who came to Portsmouth as French Consul in 1782.

He lived first at the Purcell boarding house, where John Paul Jones and other distinguished men also lived.

Fig. 145

EDWARD CUTTS HOUSE (1810) CHRISTIAN SHORE, PORTSMOUTH

This attractive house, of the late mansion type, was built by Edward Cutts, son of Capt. Samuel Cutts. His paternal grandsire was Richard Cutts, owner of Cutts Island in Kittery, while his maternal grandfather was Rev. Edward Holyoke, President of Harvard College.

Fig. 146

EDWARD CUTTS HOUSE—ENTRANCE ON THE COACH ROAD

Fig. 147

Edward Cutts House—Side Entrance on hill, with ramped fence

Fig. 148

Jones Street (now Prospect Street), Portsmouth

On the Map of 1813 this street is called "Jones Street", and the records show that one of the earliest owners, perhaps the builder of the corner house, was William Jones. There are no further records. The bareness of this high windswept little street with no sidewalks, and with three of its early houses still standing in a row gives a picture of the uncompromising aspect of early New England life.

Fig. 149

Old Cemetery (1754) Portsmouth

This typical New England "Burying-Ground" reaches from Pleasant Street to the water.

Fig. 150

Dead End—Franklin Street, Portsmouth

This quaint little street leading down to the South Mill Pond was called "Coltar Lane" many years ago. The house on the right, nearest the pond, numbered 37, is the home of Mr. Oscar Laighton, brother of Celia Laighton Thaxter, the poetess. It was once the home of James Moses, an architect and builder.

Fig. 151

Hand wrought iron eagle on cemetery gate at Hampton, N. H. Date unknown.

Fig. 152

Joshua Wentworth House (1770) Hanover Street, opposite Fleet Street, Portsmouth

Col. Joshua Wentworth built this house. He was an officer in the 1st N. H. Regiment; a member of Congress, and Commissary for the Army and Navy during the Revolution. Later he built himself a new house on Middle Street which was removed in 1813 by his son-in-law, Samuel Larkin, who built the Larkin-Rice house on the same site. While Col. Wentworth was residing here, Gov. John Hancock, his lady and their son were entertained by him, and young Hancock delighted the Portsmouth dignitaries by dancing the minuet for them.

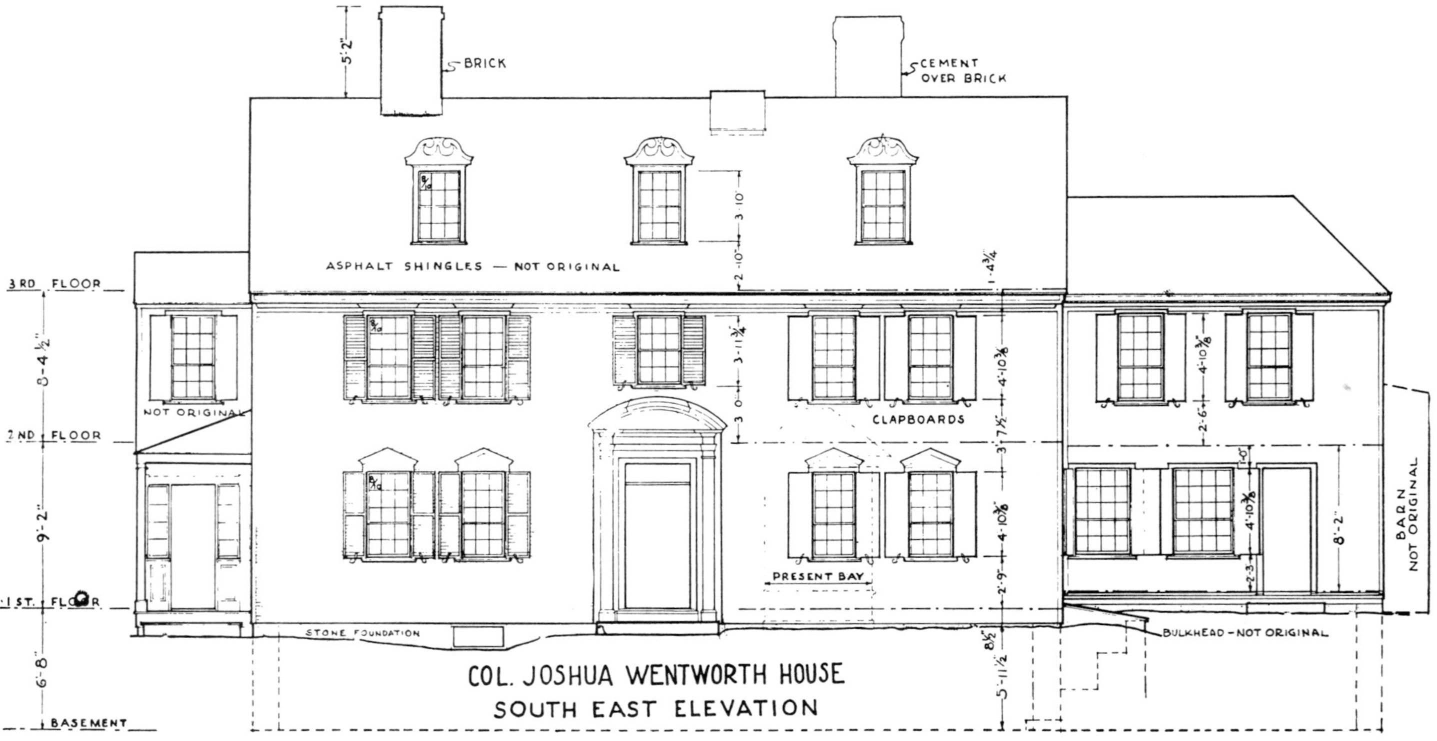

Fig. 153

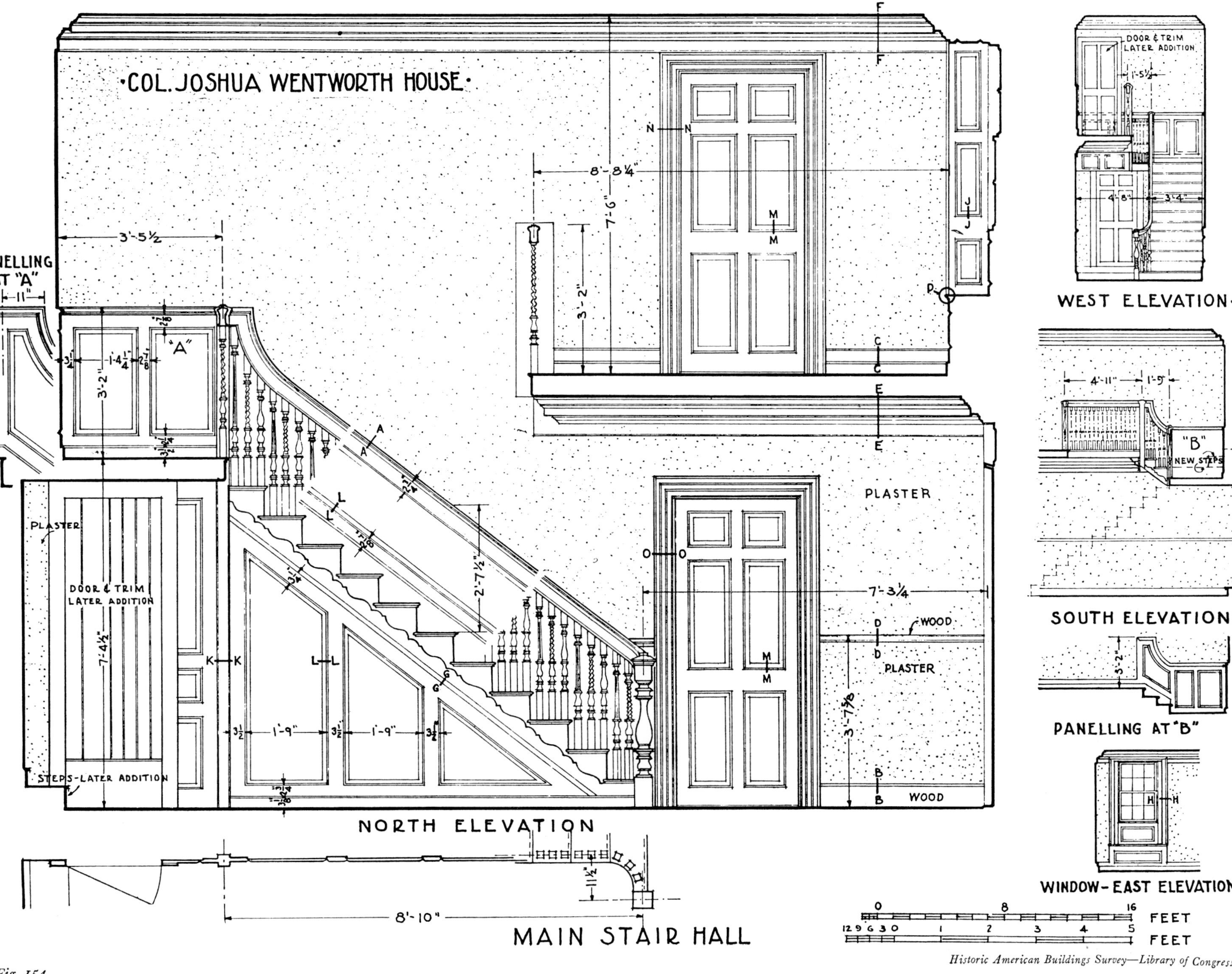

Historic American Buildings Survey—Library of Congress

Fig. 154

·COL. JOSHUA WENTWORTH HOUSE·
TURNED
SQ
DOTTED LINE IS ℄ OF LOW POINT
SQUARE
UPPER PART OF BALUSTERS
TURNED
SHAFTS FIT HERE
SQ
TURNED
7¼"
SQ
LOWER PART OF BALUSTERS
SHAFTS AT SECOND FLOOR MOHOGANY SHAFTS ON TREADS
BALUSTERS – MAIN STAIR HALL •
1 ¾ ½ ¼ 0 1 2 3 4 INCHES

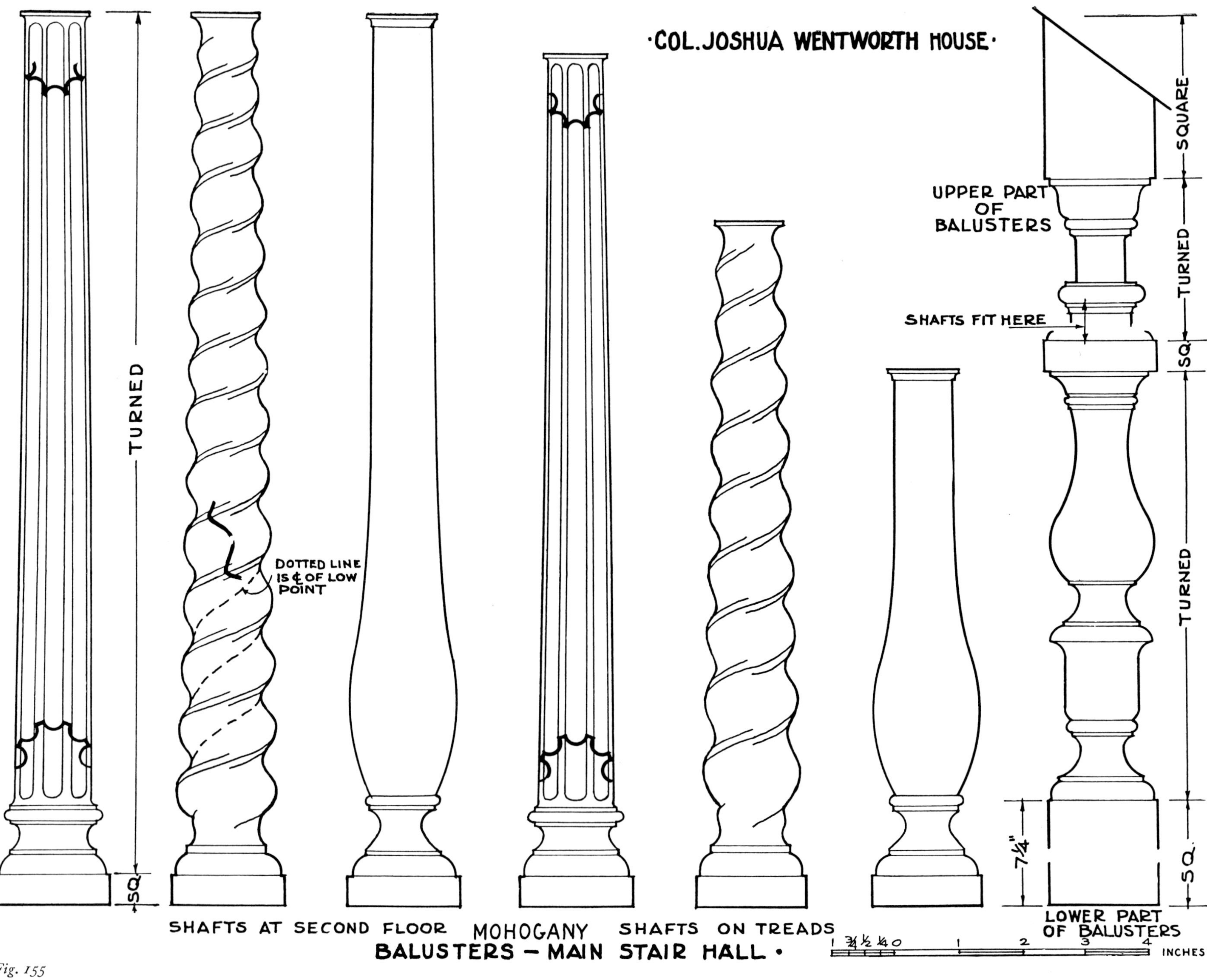

Fig. 155

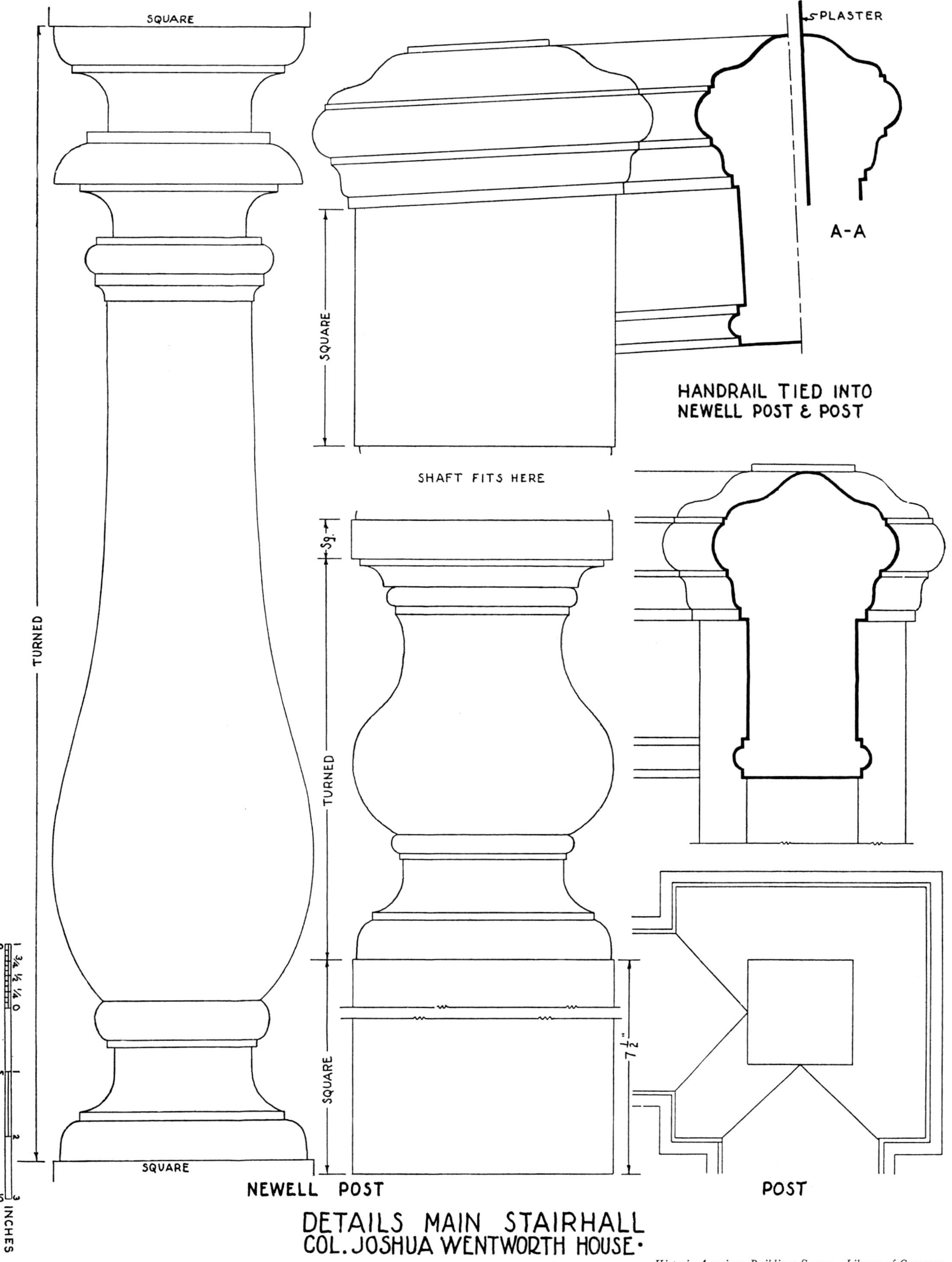

Historic American Buildings Survey—Library of Congress

Fig. 156

Fig. 157

Colonel Paul Wentworth House (1701) Salmon Falls, N. H.

This comes close to being a seventeenth century house. It was built in 1701 by Col. Paul Wentworth, grandson of Elder William, the first of this numerous family in this country. Col. Wentworth was in the lumber business and only the choicest pine boards were used in his house. He was married in 1704 and brought his bride to this house, considered the finest in the vicinity. A secret door in the kitchen floor leads to a small sub-cellar where the family sought refuge in Indian attacks.

In 1936 this house was removed to Belmont, Mass. by Mr. and Mrs. Frederic Blodgett, the present owners. Mr. Blodgett is a Wentworth descendant.

Fig. 158 *From "Old Time New England" Courtesy of the Society for the Preservation of New England Antiquities*

COLONEL PAUL WENTWORTH HOUSE

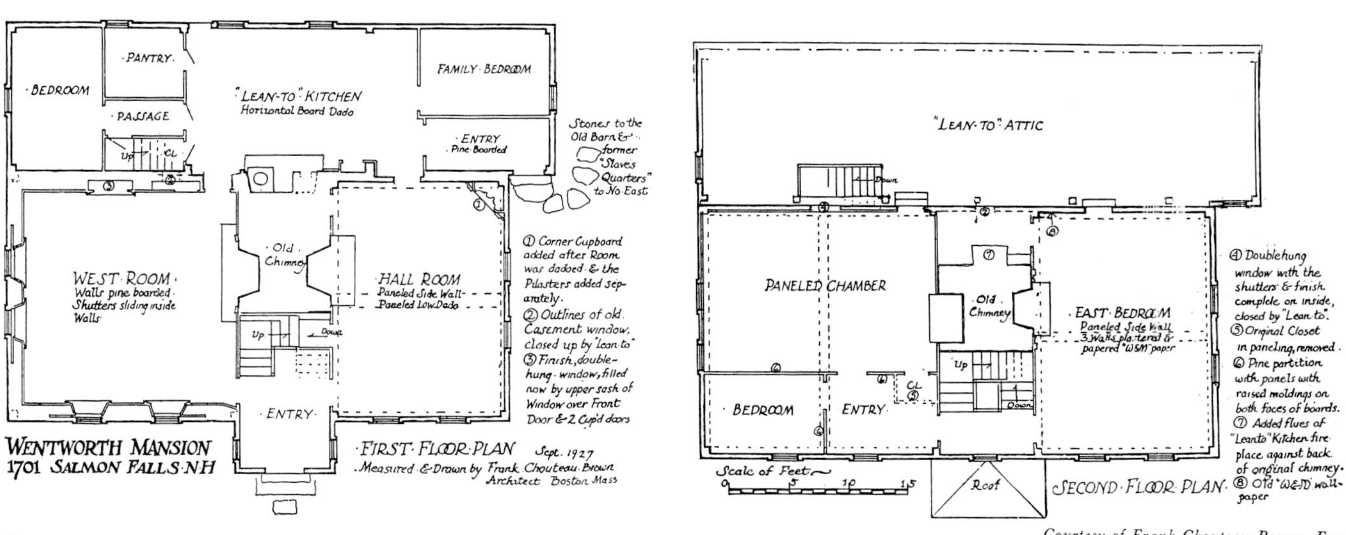

Fig. 159 *Courtesy of Frank Chouteau Brown, Esq.*

Fig. 160

ROBERT FOLLETT HOUSE (CIRCA 1767) KITTERY POINT, MAINE

This drawing room about 18′ x 30′ shows early panelling on the chimney side of the room. The ceiling shows a summerbeam 30′ long down the center. This seems a difficult and unintelligent manner of framing, and must have been the result of habit rather than thought.

Fig. 161

1798 HOUSE—KITTERY POINT, MAINE

This long one and one-half story house with three chimneys and without dormers is an unspoiled example of early work. It is painted red with white trim which must have been its color for many years.

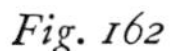

Fig. 162

Photographs by Arthur C. Haskell

Fig. 163

Frost Garrison (1738) East Eliot, Maine
(originally Kittery, Mass. before its separation from Maine)

The largest local garrison. The immense girders, plates and sills are squared pine tree trunks. Beneath wall paper in the dwelling (1732) have been found beautifully stencilled patterns in color (see Fig. 299).

Fig. 164

Corner Cupboard in Robert Follett House

This is a good example of a cupboard of this type. The upper part of the door is without panels. The front curve of every shelf is on a diminishing pattern.

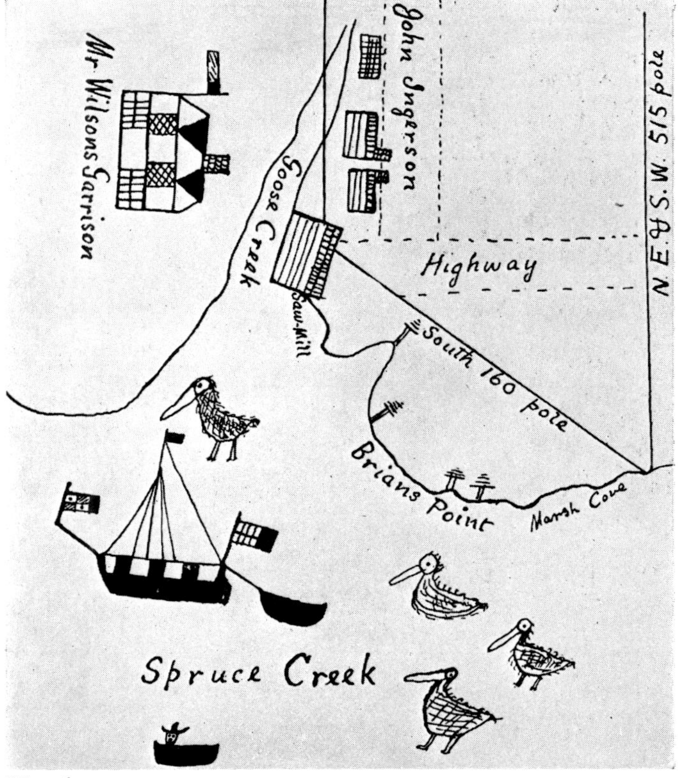

Fig. 165

Map of Goose Cove (1696) Kittery Point, Maine

The geese, the sloop, and the boatman in a wide puritan hat—also, and more important, a well drawn Jacobean house, were traced from the town records.

Fig. 166

WILLIAM PEPPERRELL HOUSE (1682) KITTERY POINT, MAINE

The House built by Col. Pepperrell, father of Sir William, in 1682 surpassed in grandeur any residence in the province.

Sir William added about fifteen feet to each end of it, and these additions were taken away by a subsequent owner. It originally had "a sharp roof."

Fig. 167

THE BRAY HOUSE (1662) KITTERY POINT, MAINE

This is the oldest house in Kittery. Here Court was held in the old days before County Buildings were known.

Fig. 168

TOMB OF COLONEL WILLIAM PEPPERRELL AND FAMILY (1736) KITTERY POINT, MAINE

This tomb was cut in London by the order of his son, Sir William in 1736 at a cost of thirty-four pounds, eleven shillings and four pence. It was erected in the middle of the Great Orchard and stands beautifully today on a mound surrounded by a circle of evergreens. Vestiges of small burials near it seem to be those of his slaves.

Fig. 169

WILLIAM PEPPERRELL HOUSE—GREAT STAIR HALL

This is the widest and deepest stair landing that the writer has observed in any early house. The stair window looked out on the "Great Orchard" of Sir William's day.

Fig. 170

William Pepperrell House—View of Great Stair Landing from Above

This landing is as large as an ordinary room.

Fig. 171

William Pepperrell House—Panelled Work in West Drawing Room

The rolled moulding around the fireplace and that around the door recalls the similar work in the Macpheadris-Warner house.

Fig. 172

OLD PARSONAGE AT KITTERY POINT, MAINE (1729-30)

The first minister was Rev. John Newmarch, who graduated from Harvard in the Class of 1690. He preached in two places and lived at a point between them, in a house surrounded by earthworks, the remains of which are still visible. When he rode on his rounds he carried arms against Indian attack. His body was exhumed and transferred to the cemetery of his church in 1936.

Fig. 173

OLD PULPIT AT KITTERY POINT, MAINE (1730)

This pulpit, part of the original church, was removed in the 1870's. Fortunately, it was stored in a barn and re-installed about 1900.

Fig. 174

MAPLEWOOD AVE., CHRISTIAN SHORE, NORTH STREET, PORTSMOUTH

House No. 273, was formerly No. 9 North Street. It was early the home of James White, a ship's carpenter, who was employed in the Raynes shipyard. He may have been the builder.

Fig. 175

WATERHOUSE HOUSE (1700) CHRISTIAN SHORE, MAPLEWOOD AVE., PORTSMOUTH

This house was built at Freeman's Point (then called Ham's Point). It was built by Timothy Waterhouse, a tanner. About 1765 the old house was moved down to its present location.

Fig. 176

Fig. 177

Colonel Nathaniel Meserve House (1740) Maplewood Ave., Portsmouth (sometimes called Boyd-Raynes House)

In 1740 this house was built by Nathaniel Meserve, a shipbuilder and Colonel in the British army. His shipyard was directly in the rear of the house, and here he built a number of vessels for the British navy. His widow sold the property to Col. George Boyd, who enlarged it and laid out extensive grounds which extended as far south as the present depot. At the outbreak of the Revolution Col. Boyd retired to England. In 1787 he felt that the time had come to take up his residence in Portsmouth once more, so he started for New England, bringing with him an elegant coach and an English coachman, and the most elaborate tombstone he could procure. The tombstone may be seen today in the old North Cemetery.

The estate was purchased by George Raynes, who will probably go down in history as Portsmouth's most famous shipbuilder. From 1832 to 1855, about seventy ships were launched from his shipyard.

Until recent years there was an intricate Chinese balustrade and "whale-walk," enclosing the second chimney—marking the centre of Boyd-Raynes House. (See plan)

GEORGE RAYNES
1832
GEORGE BOYD
1768-1787
WILLIAM BOYD
1787-1832
FIRST FLOOR
SECOND FLOOR
THIRD FLOOR
NATHANIAL MESERVE
1740-
PETER LIVIUS
-1768
SUPPLEMENTARY DRAWING
SHOWING THE THREE STAGES OF THE DEVELOPMENT
BOYD-RAYNES HOUSE
4 0 24 48 72 FEET

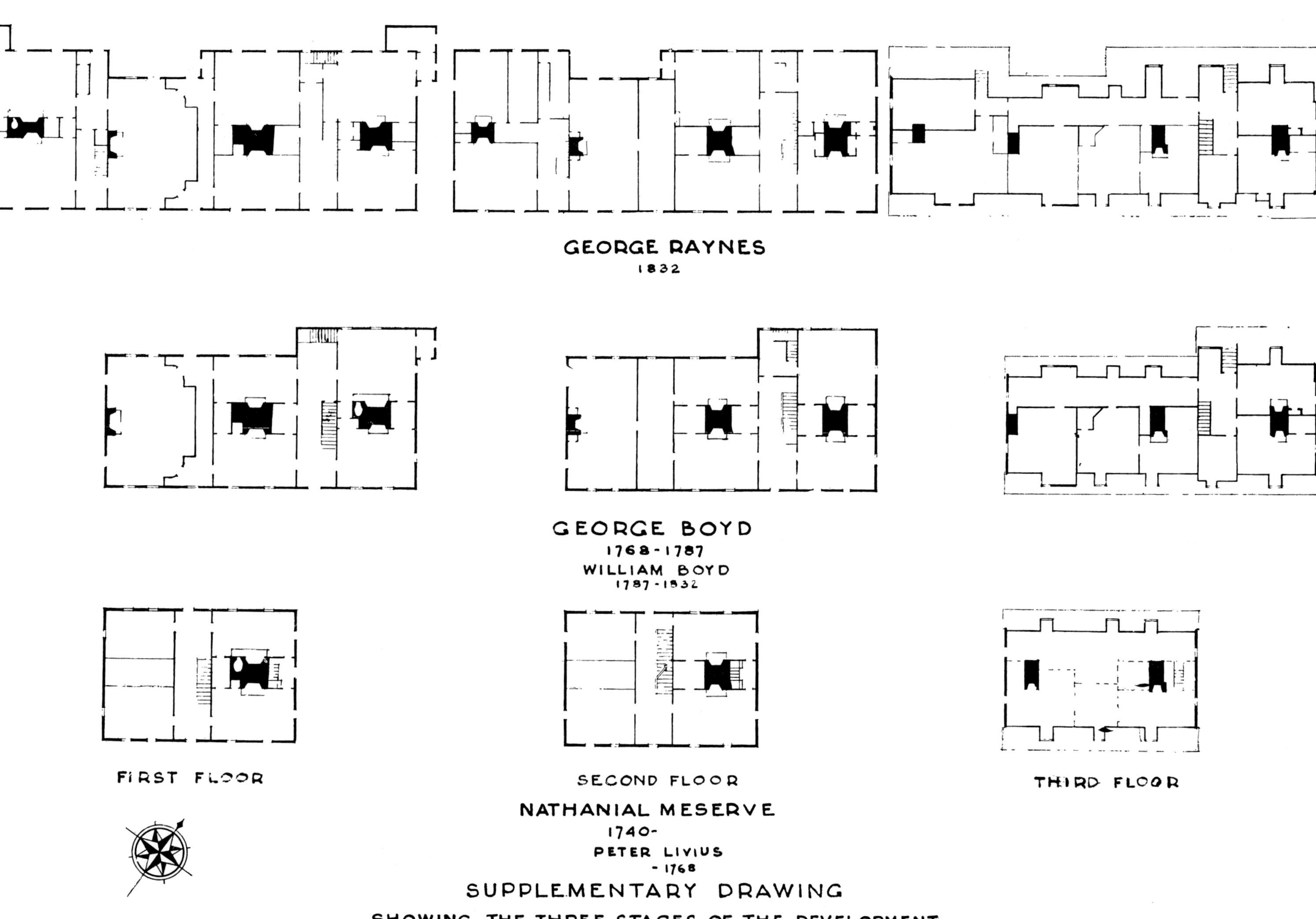

Fig. 178

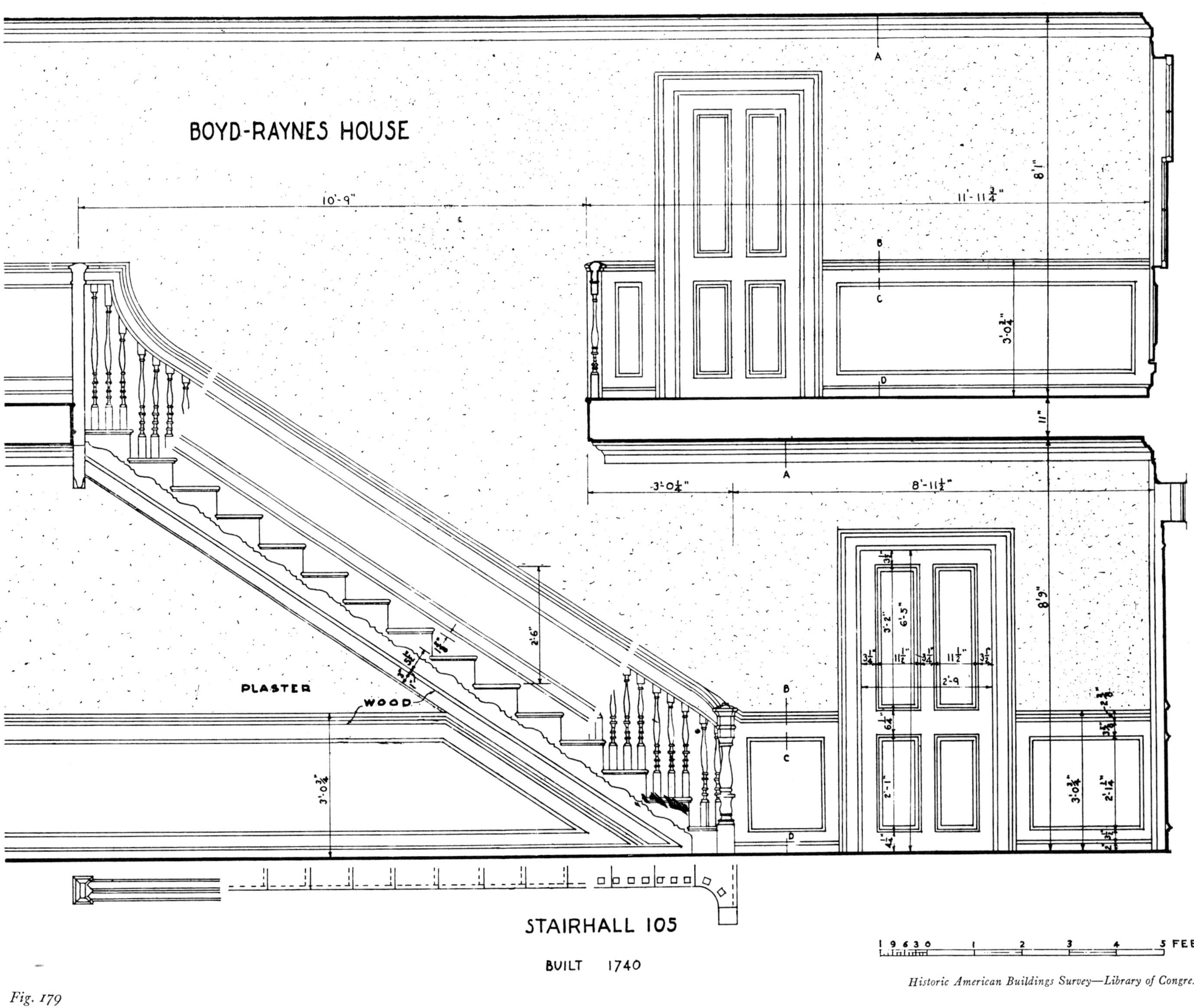

Historic American Buildings Survey—Library of Congress

Fig. 179

BOYD-RAYNES HOUSE
DETAIL NEWEL POST H105
TURNED
SQ
TURNED
SQUARE
7½"
1 ¾ ½ ¼ 0 1 2 3 INCHES
SQUARE
TURNED

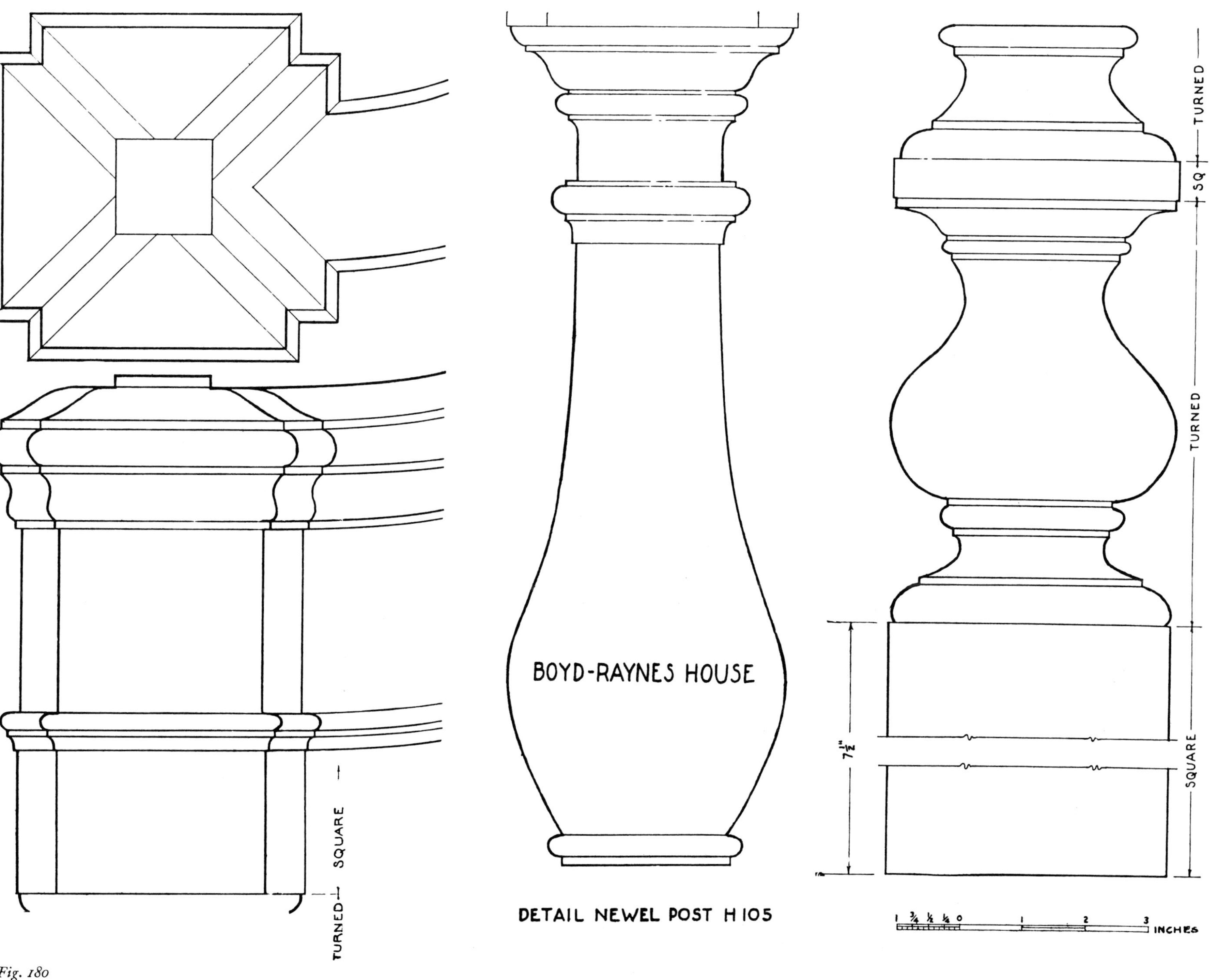

Fig. 180

ROOF LINE
PLAN
FINIAL
TURNED
SQUARE
LEAD FLASHING
WARPED SURFACE
THIS FACIA IS ONE BOARD FROM CORNICE TO RIDGE. SCROLL & URN IS APPLIED AGAINST THIS BOARD & CIRCLE IS 'V' CUT IN.
SCROLL
BOYD RAYNES HOUSE
DORMER DETAIL
BUILT 1740
1 ¾ ½ ¼ 0 1 2 3 INCHES

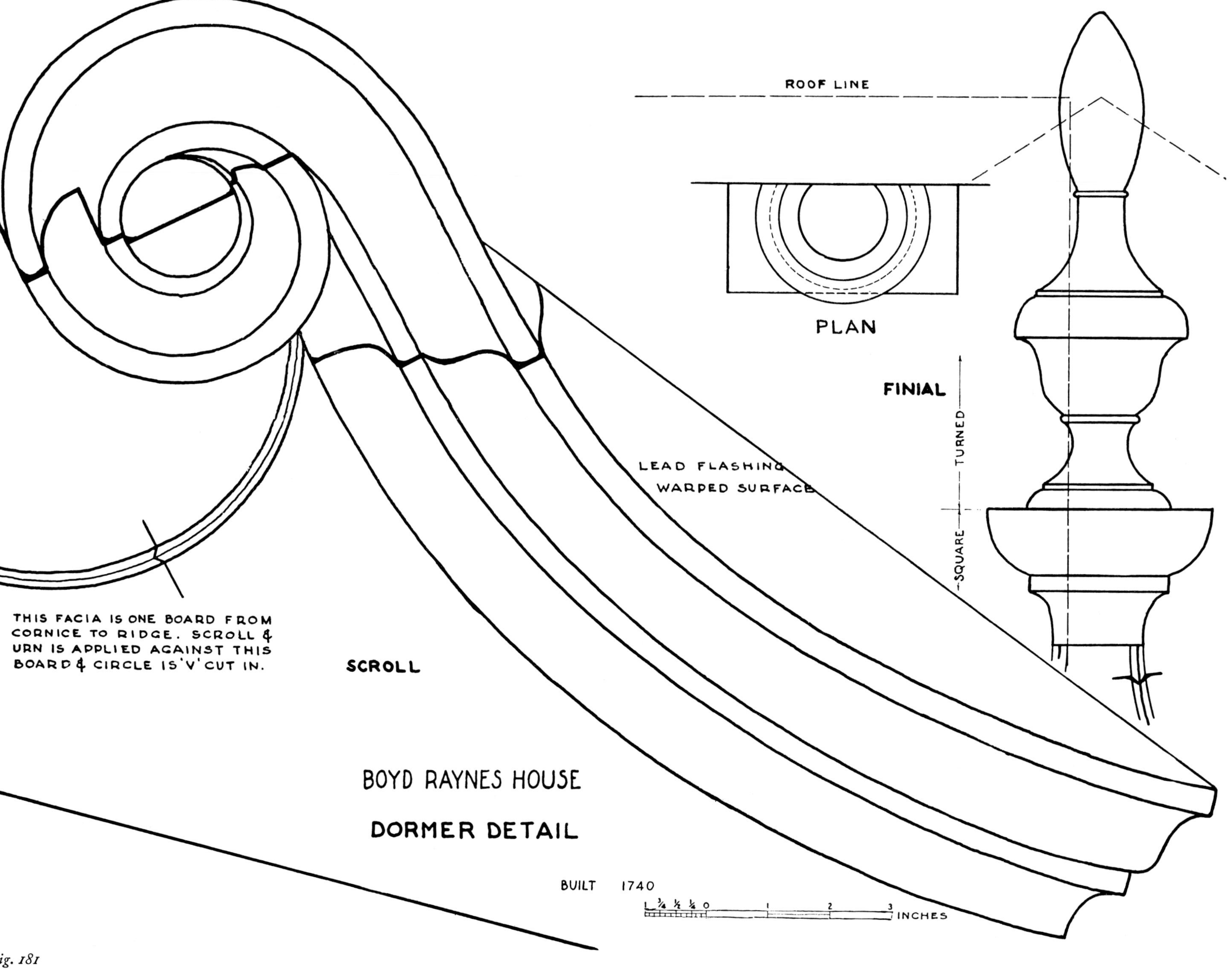

Fig. 181

BOYD-RAYNES HOUSE
DETAILS OF DORMERS
WIDE MUNTINS FOUND IN THREE DORMERS ON REAR IN LONG BACK HALL - CENTRAL PORTION
MUNTINS
JAMB
CORNICE
SASH
FACIA BOARD ON CHEEKS
SILL
1"
SHINGLES
GAMBREL MOULD IS A CONTINUATION OF THE DORMER CROWN MOULD
CLAPBOARDS
SIDE
1'-7⅛"
5"
1½"
3-10½
6'-9"
2'-4"
SECTION
8/10
3'-10½"
3'-0"
2'-4⅜"
ELEVATION

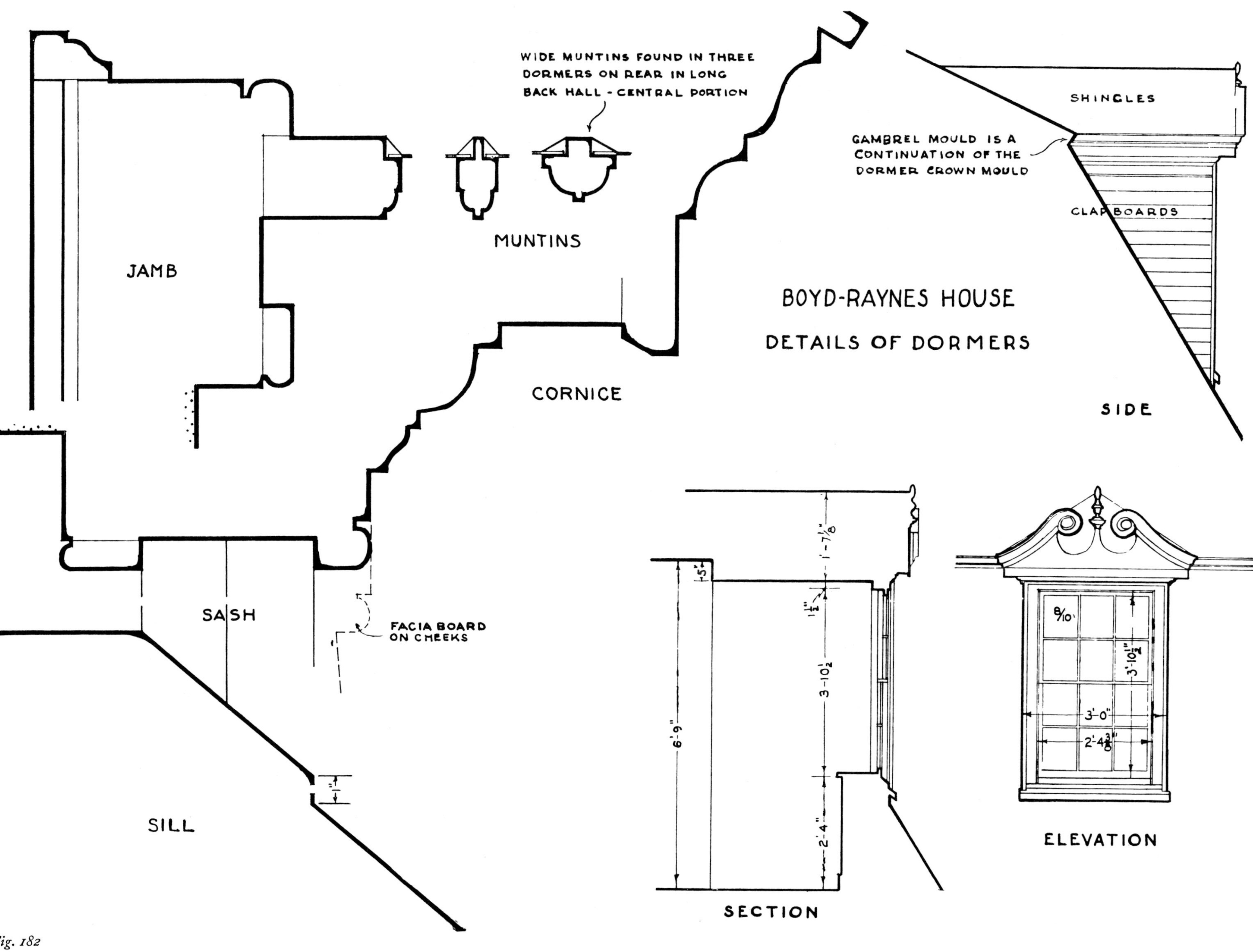

Fig. 182

ELEVATION
W. I. STRAP HINGE
BOYD-RAYNES HOUSE
TOP VIEW
DETAILS OF SMOKE CHAMBER ROOM 301
3RD FLOOR
BUILT 1740
ROUND
ELEVATION
W. I. LATCH
W. I. HOOKS
6-HOOKS 6"± O.C
TOP VIEW
FULL SIZE
BRICK
CEILING
FLUE
OUTER DOOR WOOD AS DETAILED.
INNER DOOR 2" PLANK NO HINGES.
FLOOR
OUTER DOOR
PLAN
3/4" = 1'-0"
END ELEVATIONS

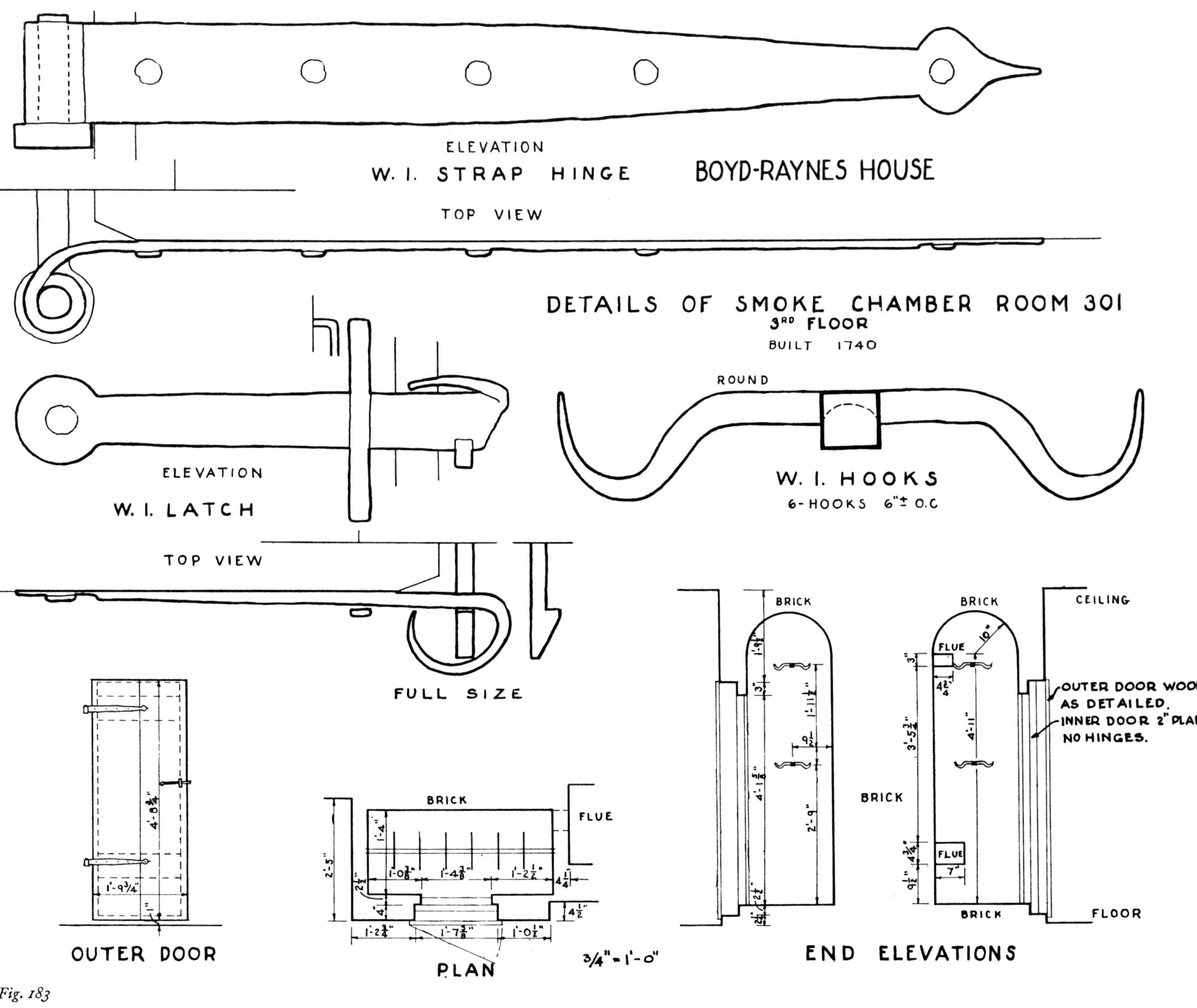

Fig. 183

Fig. 184

Jackson House (1664) Northwest Street, Christian Shore, Portsmouth

The original owner of this house was John Jackson who came to Portsmouth in 1645, from Dartmouth, England and settled here. When he died he left his "House and lot and 100 pounds to his son Richard." This house is owned by the N. E. Society for the Preservation of Antiquities. The very early interior is of great interest to the antiquarian and to the architect.

Fig. 185

The Dam-Drew Garrison House (1675) Dover, N. H.

A true Garrison House or fort for defense against the Indians. When an attack was expected, the original wood roof was covered with turf. Log cabin construction was not commonly used in earliest New England, as some have assumed, and then only used for forts.

This building is here shown in its original strategic position on a little rise at Dover Point. Now removed to Woodman Institute, Dover.

Fig. 186

OLD PARSONAGE AT NEWINGTON, N. H. (1710)

It is said that at the time this parsonage was dedicated, there were nine members and the town made a fast day of the event. The first minister was Rev. Joseph Adams, uncle of the second president of the United States. His pastorate lasted 68 years, and his salary was eighty pounds a year.

Fig. 187

SEAVEY HOUSE (1730) RYE, N. H.

It is believed to have been built by William Seavey, an early settler of the town, in 1730.

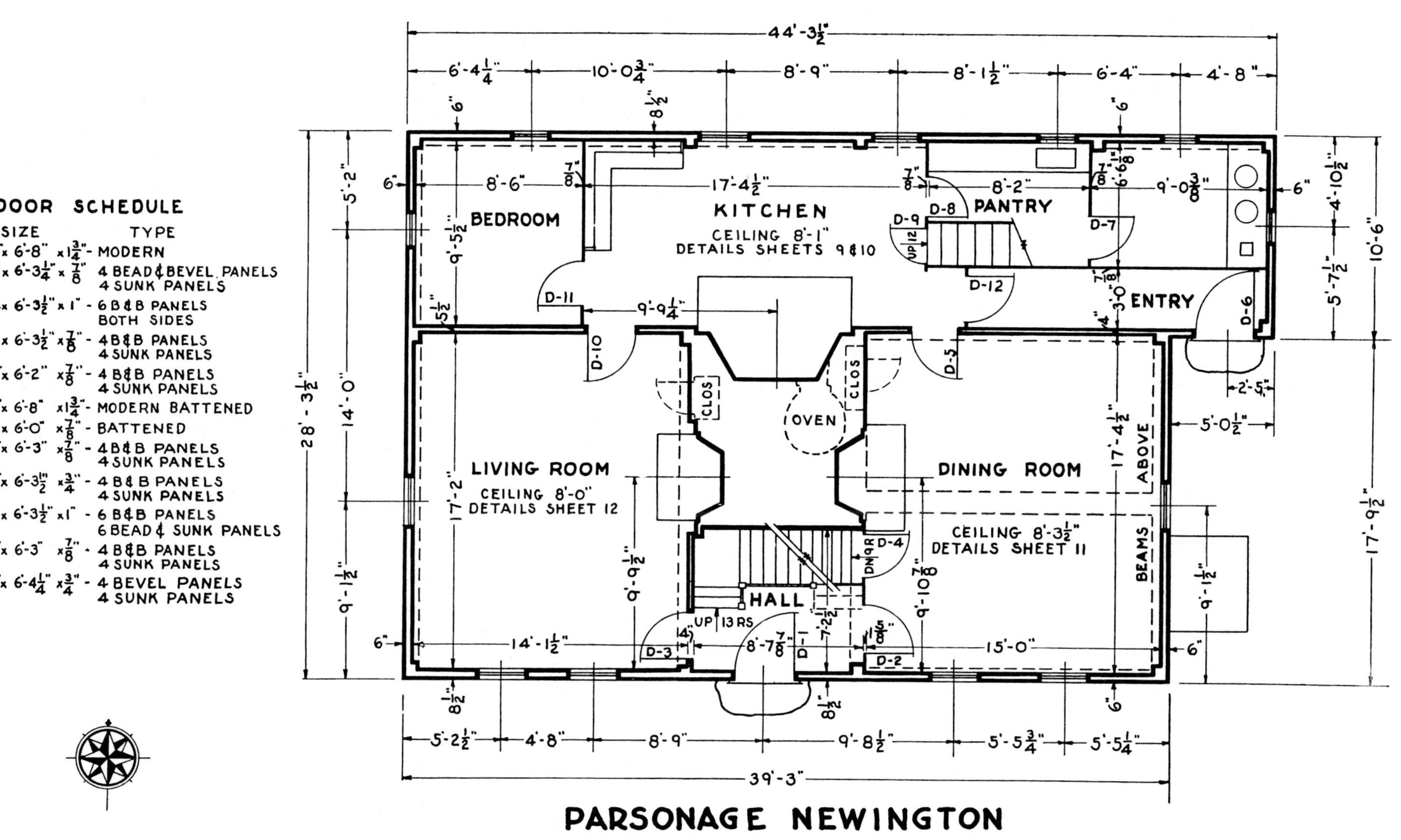

Historic American Buildings Survey—Library of Congress

DOOR SCHEDULE

NO	SIZE	TYPE
D-1	3'-0⅞" x 6'-8" x 1¾"	MODERN
D-2	2'-5" x 6'-3¼" x ⅞"	4 BEAD & BEVEL PANELS 4 SUNK PANELS
D-3	2'-5" x 6'-3½" x 1"	6 B & B PANELS BOTH SIDES
D-4	2'-4" x 6'-3½" x ⅞"	4 B & B PANELS 4 SUNK PANELS
D-5	2'-3¾" x 6'-2" x ⅞"	4 B & B PANELS 4 SUNK PANELS
D-6	3'-0¾" x 6'-8" x 1¾"	MODERN BATTENED
D-7	2'-3" x 6'-0" x ⅞"	BATTENED
D-8	2'-2¼" x 6'-3" x ⅞"	4 B & B PANELS 4 SUNK PANELS
D-9	1'-11¼" x 6'-3½" x ¾"	4 B & B PANELS 4 SUNK PANELS
D-10	2'-5" x 6'-3½" x 1"	6 B & B PANELS 6 BEAD & SUNK PANELS
D-11	2'-4½" x 6'-3" x ⅞"	4 B & B PANELS 4 SUNK PANELS
D-12	2'-5½" x 6'-4¼" x ¾"	4 BEVEL PANELS 4 SUNK PANELS

Fig. 188

PARSONAGE NEWINGTON
MAIN STAIR HALL
STAIR GIRT
MODERN CEILING
MODERN MATCHED BOARDS
ATTIC FLOOR
D-22
D-20
D-21
D-3
D-2
NOTE:-
RISERS 8½" ±
TREADS 7" ±
WEST ELEVATION
NORTH ELEVATION
EAST ELEVATION

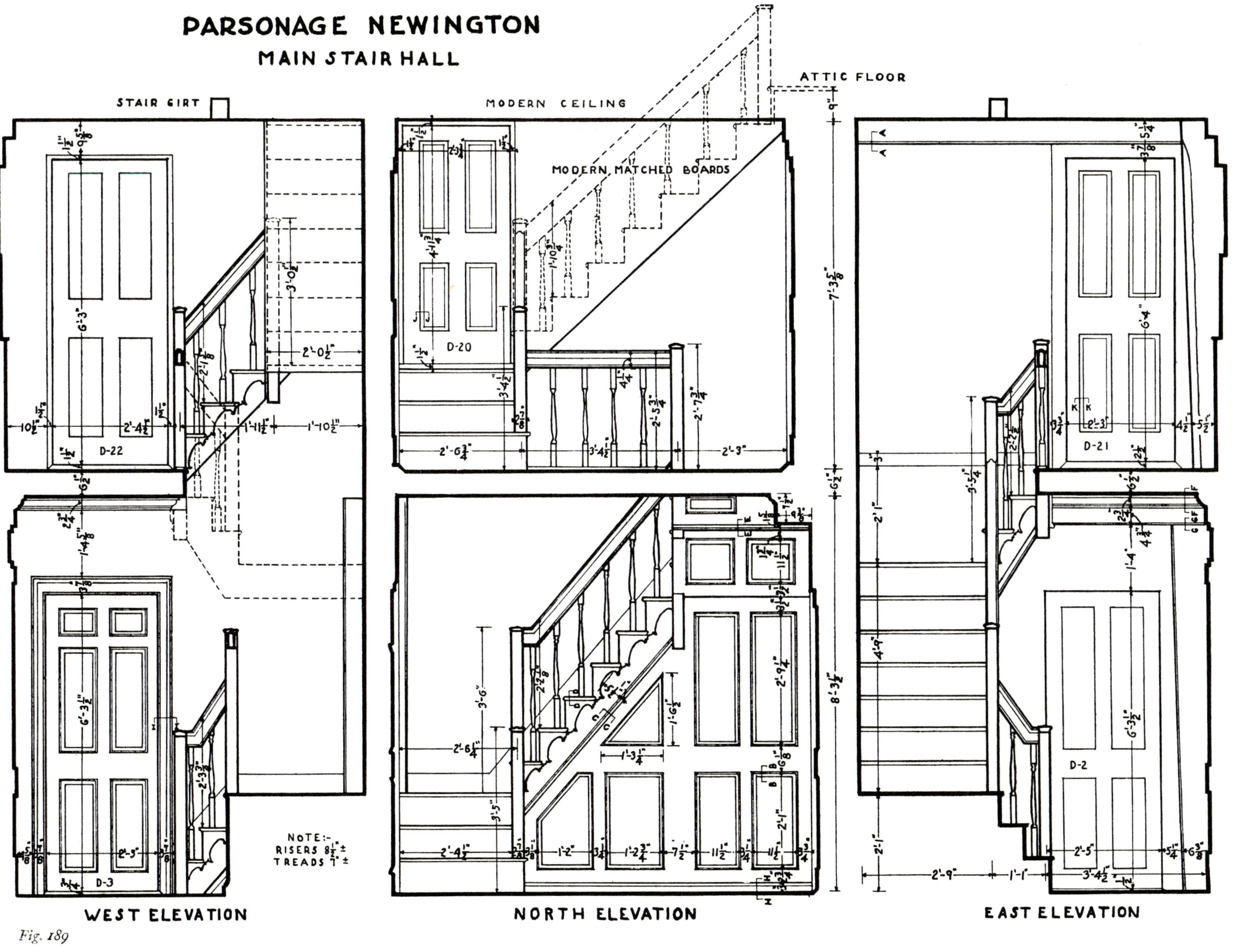

Fig. 189

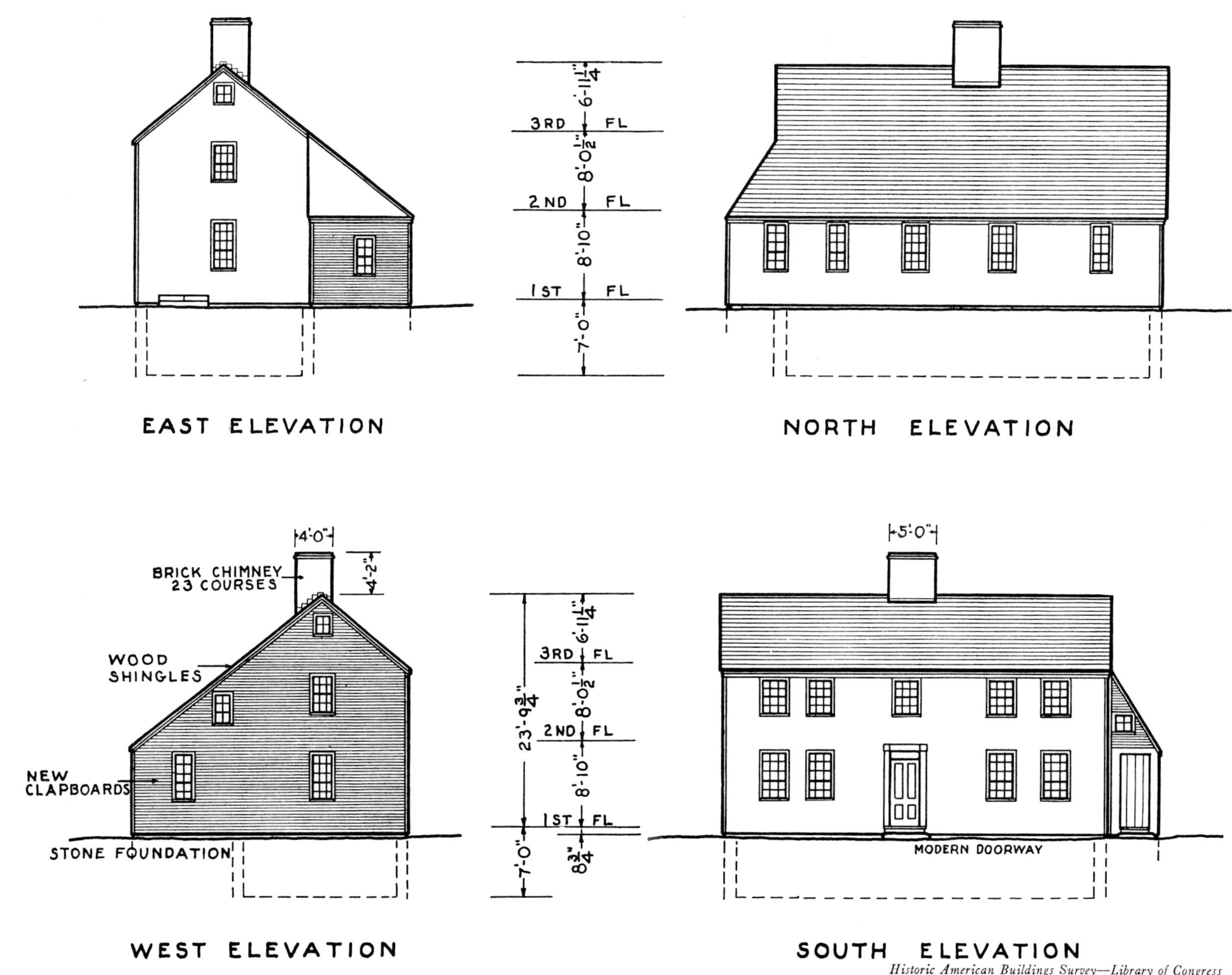

Historic American Buildings Survey—Library of Congress

Fig. 190

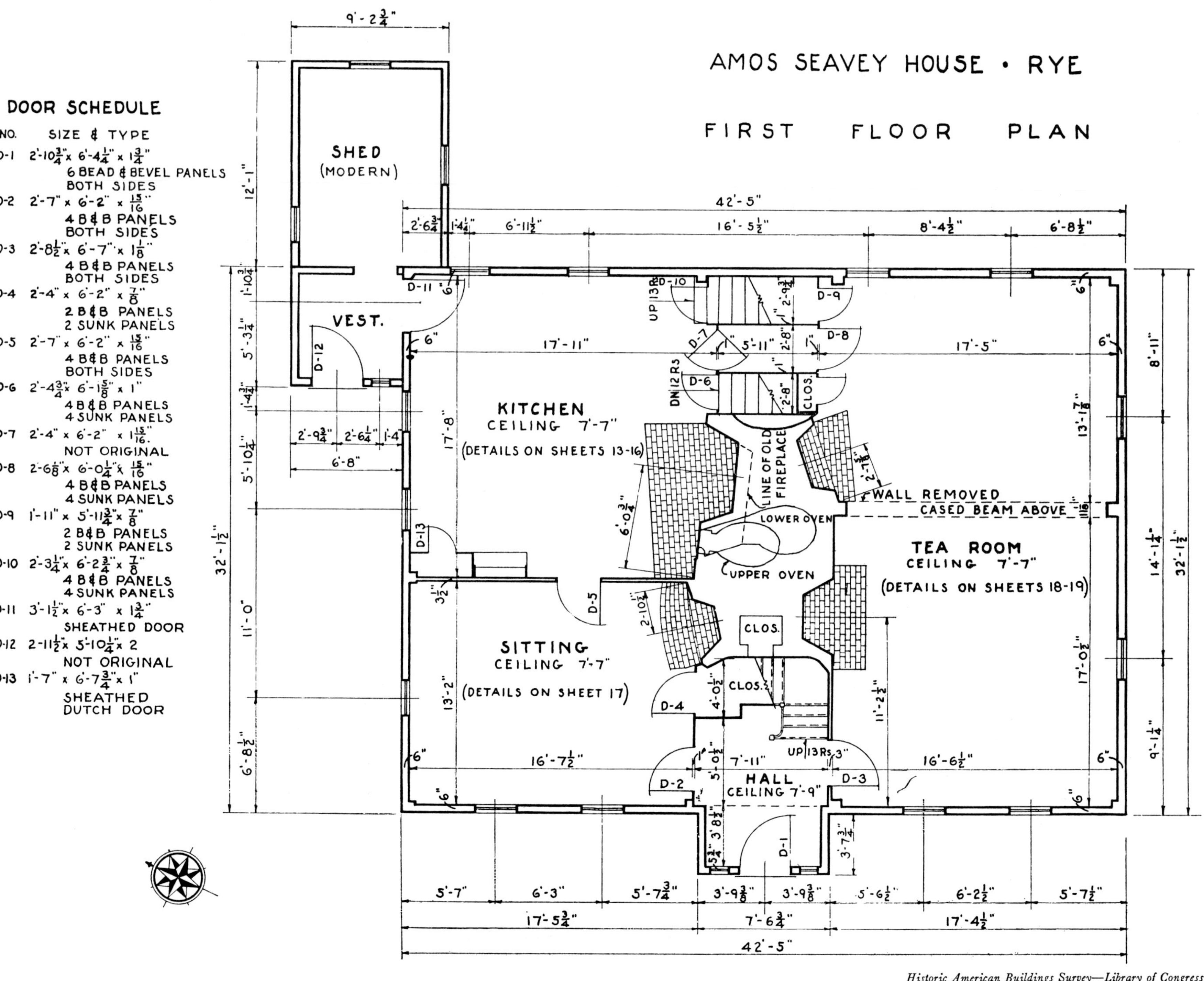

Fig. 191

Historic American Buildings Survey—Library of Congress

AMOS SEAVEY HOUSE
STAIR HALL
PLASTER
D-21
D-3
WOOD
LANDING
NOT VERTICAL DIMENSION
NORTHWEST ELEVATION
NORTHEAST ELEVATION
SOUTHEAST ELEVATION
NOTE STAIR RAIL NOT PARALLEL TO LINE OF NOSING

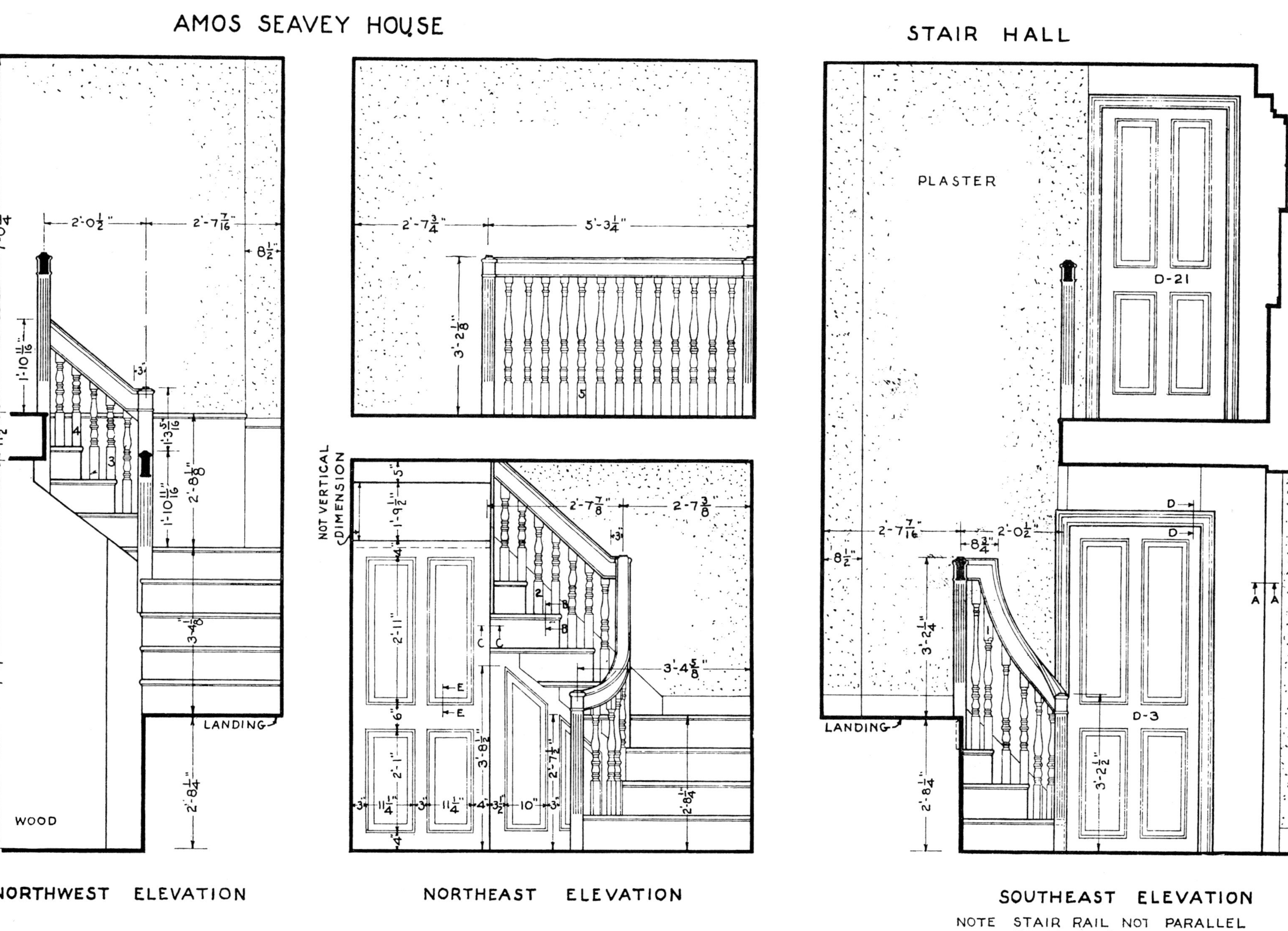

Fig. 192

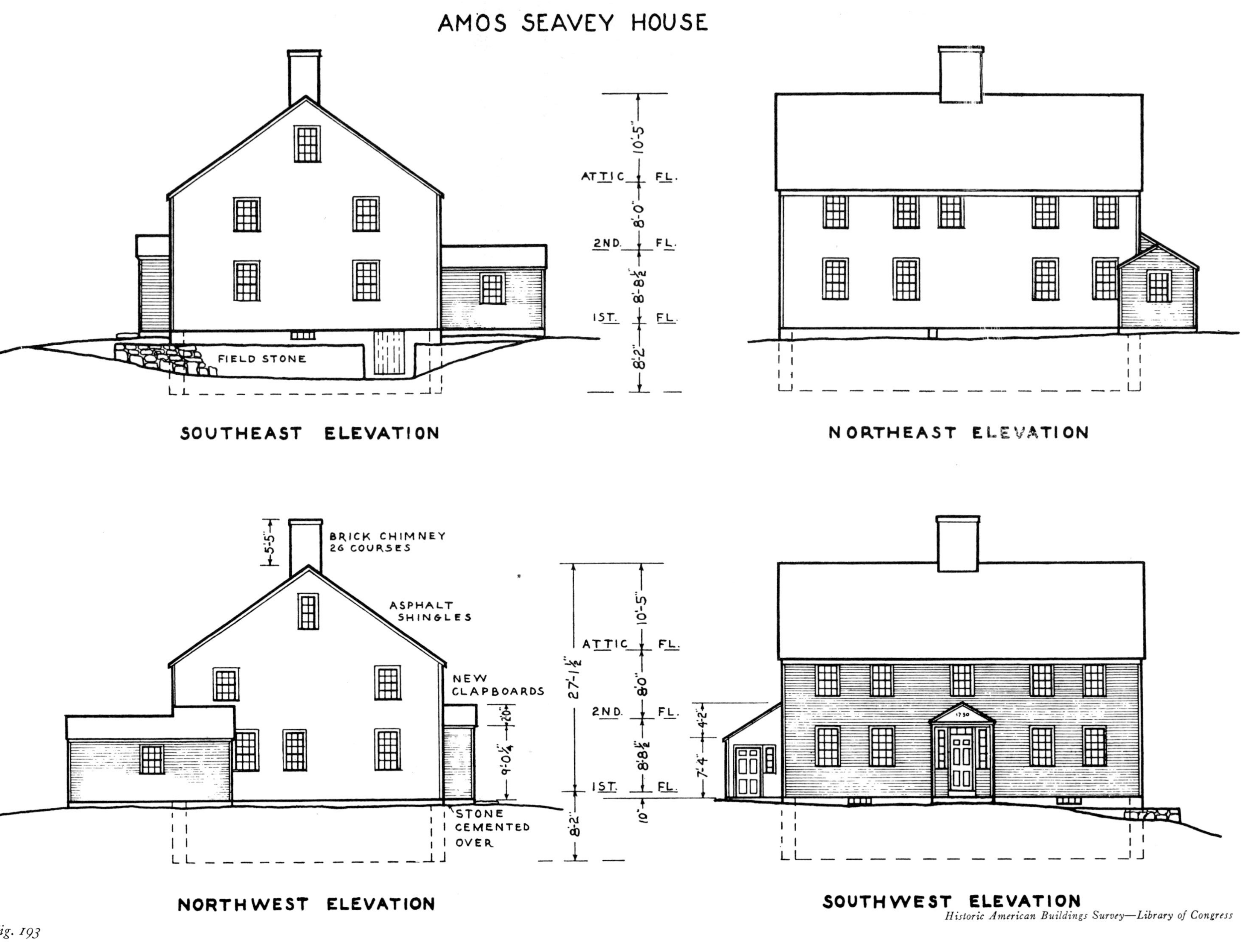

Historic American Buildings Survey—Library of Congress

Fig. 193

Fig. 194

CONANT HOUSE, WASHINGTON STREET COR. JEFFERSON, PORTSMOUTH

This is doubtless a very old house, but no records are found regarding the date. The only record we have is that it was occupied by one Aaron Conant, the Boston Stage driver. It has a fine old chimney—with an odd hump in the roof around it.

Fig. 195

JABEZ FITCH HOUSE (POSSIBLY 17TH CENTURY) HIGH STREET, PORTSMOUTH

This house was the residence of the Rev. Jabez Fitch, pastor of the North Parish in 1725. Since the chimney is of a very early type, the house was possibly built before 1700.

Fig. 196

COTTON HOUSE, 144 WASHINGTON STREET, PORTSMOUTH

The date of this house is not known. It was the home of Leonard Cotton who went to Trinidad where he became a prosperous merchant, and came back to Portsmouth. No construction date has been found.

It was possibly built by Leonard's grandfather, Nathaniel Cotton, the "Housesmith" about 1760, as well as the Laighton House at Washington and Gates.

The entrance porch steps are evidently a later addition.

Fig. 197

Tobias Lear House (Circa 1740) Hunking Street, Portsmouth

The Lear house adjoining Wentworth-Gardner was built by the third Tobias Lear, grandfather of Colonel Lear, who for sixteen years was private secretary to General Washington.

This severe and rather stately early type house is famous as one of those visited by Washington, who came to pay his respects to Madam Lear, mother of Tobias. Lear's second and third wives were both nieces of Mrs. Washington.

Fig. 198

PURCELL HOUSE (1757-1759) STATE STREET, PORTSMOUTH

This house is believed to have been built by Capt. Gregory Purcell. The old Rockingham County deeds show that he purchased the land from Capt. Nathaniel Peirce in 1757. He was married in 1759 to Miss Sarah Wentworth, niece of Gov. Benning Wentworth, so it is probable that the house was built during those years, for this was his home until his death in 1776.

After Capt. Purcell's death, his widow conducted a boarding house here, and among her boarders were Capt. John Paul Jones, and M. Jean Joseph Marie Toscan, French Consul to New Hampshire. One of John Paul Jones' biographers has said that the happiest hours of his life were those spent in Portsmouth. He spent many hours in serious study of naval methods and procedure, and it is not hard to imagine the little captain treading the paths of Madame Purcell's garden in the cool of the evening.

The house was purchased by the Portsmouth Historical Society, and opened officially July 21, 1920. It is open daily during the summer months.

Fig. 199

Austin-Lyman House (1782) 27 Austin Street, Portsmouth

This charming old house was built in 1782 by the Austin family from whom the street takes its name. It has a delightful garden and is itself an almost faultless example of this Early American Georgian type.

Fig. 200

Richard Tibbetts House, 212 Pleasant Street, Portsmouth

The exact date of this house is not known. One record shows that it was sold in 1774.

Fig. 201

Timothy Upham House, 199 Middle Street, Portsmouth

This house is shown on the Map of 1813.

Fig. 202

CHASE HOUSE (CIRCA 1730) COURT STREET, PORTSMOUTH

This was the home of William Chase, a merchant. It was at one time a Children's home.

Fig. 203

JOHN LAIGHTON HOUSE, 278 COURT STREET, PORTSMOUTH

The date is unknown, but in 1795 this house was purchased by Deacon Tappan from Miss Nabby Chase, who had doubtless lived in it for some time.

Fig. 204

BAILEY-ALDRICH HOUSE (1790) 386 COURT STREET, PORTSMOUTH

This house was owned and occupied by Thomas Darling Bailey, grandfather of Thomas Bailey Aldrich, to whom it is now a memorial.

Fig. 205

SEAVEY-PARKER HOUSE (1790) 56 ISLINGTON STREET, PORTSMOUTH

This house was first lived in by William Seavey who built it.

Fig. 206

REMICK HOUSE (1696) 49 ISLINGTON STREET, PORTSMOUTH
(known as Jenny Stewart's House)

This very old house was build by Daniel Remark. In the 1850's carpenters discovered the following names cut in one of the beams: "Daniel Remark, John Thompson, . . . Holmes, J. Thompson, . . . Stephens and John Thomas," probably the names of those who helped Daniel Remark build his home.

Fig. 207

AYERS HOUSE, 232 COURT STREET, PORTSMOUTH

This house has ear-marks of being a very old one. It escaped the Great Fire of 1813, which had its start directly opposite.

Fig. 208

No. 47 Howard Street, Portsmouth

A good type of two story and a half, lean-to house, on a little street that has never boasted a sidewalk.

No record of construction is found. In 1827 James Drisco, shipmaster, lived there, but it was doubtless an old house in his time.

Fig. 209

Lambert House, 5 Charles Street, Portsmouth

There is no data on this house. It must be very old. Charles Street is one of the tiny streets of the ancient maritime quarter—its houses in a line, and no sidewalks.

Fig. 210

NEWCASTLE AVENUE, PORTSMOUTH

An undisturbed New England Waterfront. Of the ten houses visible all but two are old examples. No sidewalk along the houses.

Fig. 211

CAPTAIN DANIEL FERNALD HOUSE (1732) MANNING STREET COR. OF HOWARD, PORTSMOUTH

Built in 1732 by Capt. Samuel Frost, and occupied for many years by Capt. Daniel Fernald. In the war of 1812 Capt. Fernald smuggled powder for the American forces.

Fig. 212

NATHANIEL TREADWELL HOUSE (1758) 321 STATE STREET, PORTSMOUTH

Built in 1758 by Mrs. Charles Treadwell for her son Nathaniel. Afterwards it was occupied as a tavern and known as The Ark. In 1814 when Portsmouth was expecting an attack from the British, Gov. Gilman, in command of 5,000 New Hampshire militiamen, made this his headquarters.

Fig. 213

LORD HOUSE, 19 HOWARD STREET, PORTSMOUTH

In 1839 this house was owned by the family of Ebenezer Lord, a cabinet-maker. Construction date unknown.

Fig. 214

BRIARD-DWIGHT HOUSE (1800) 314 MIDDLE STREET, PORTSMOUTH

Built soon after 1800 and owned by Capt. William A. Briard, a shipmaster, who occupied it until 1853. The center dormer is an obvious addition.

Fig. 215

CAPTAIN OLIVER BLUNT HOUSE, 349 STATE STREET, PORTSMOUTH

Capt. Oliver was another son of John Blunt, mariner, of Newcastle and built this house. Date unknown.

Fig. 216

Laighton House, Washington Street cor. Gates, Portsmouth

This odd old house is of unknown date. In early times, it was occupied by Nathaniel Cotton, who was a "joiner and housewright" and who probably built the house himself, although there are no definite records.

Fig. 217

Gerrish House, 64 Deer Street cor. High, Portsmouth

This house is shown on the map of 1813 but that is as near as we can get to its construction date.

Fig. 218

Captain William Rice House, 93 Deer Street, Portsmouth

As early as 1741 this house was owned by John Newmarch. Capt. Rice, who later lived here, was a noted sea captain and privateersman of the war of 1812. In 1814 a "Calico Party" was held at his house, and the ladies were invited to cut the dress patterns they desired from the bales of calico which one of Capt. Rice's ships had captured from the British.

Fig. 219

Hart-Treat House, Deer Street, Portsmouth

Daniel Hart who owned much property in this vicinity is said to have built this house. It was listed in the inventory of his estate in 1740. The stone steps and the small iron balcony which adorn the house were from the Old State House.

Fig. 220

VAUGHAN-EMERY HOUSE, 338 MIDDLE STREET, PORTSMOUTH

It is not an old house, having been built some fifty years ago. Notice the pronounced roof design and sweep at the eaves.

Fig. 221

CAPTAIN JOHN SALTER HOUSE (CIRCA 1800) 130 COURT STREET, PORTSMOUTH

Most of the three storied houses on Court Street were built after 1800. It is shown on the map of 1813, and was then occupied by Mr. George Manent, who very likely built it. In 1852 Capt. John E. Salter bought it. A room was formerly papered with a wall paper representing Niagara Falls, Natural Bridge, West Point, and New York Harbor. Capt. Salter purchased this in Alsace Lorraine.

Fig. 222

Plummer Dennett House, Christian Shore, Portsmouth

Plummer Dennett, carpenter and joiner, lived here in 1839. He may have built it, and the George Dennett house besides.

Fig. 223

Whitcomb House, 48 Fleet Street, Portsmouth

This house was owned in 1779 by Joseph Pitman. No construction date. In the early 1800's it was lived in by one Benjamin Whitcomb who kept a shop in the odd shaped little ell.

Fig. 224

DRISCO HOUSE—MEETING HOUSE HILL FACING THE SOUTH WARD ROOM, PORTSMOUTH

Capt. Nathaniel Pierce sold this property just after the Revolution to Capt. James Drisco, who probably built the house about 1790.

Fig. 225

SPENCE HOUSE, 340 STATE STREET COR. FLEET, PORTSMOUTH

This is an early house, but the construction date cannot be found. In 1766 Robert Traill, a native of the Orkney Islands, lived here. A descendant married Keith Spence, who was an ancestor of James Russell Lowell.

Fig. 226

HOWELL HOUSE, 135 RICHARDS AVENUE, PORTSMOUTH

There are no records on this house. It was probably built soon after the street was opened in 1800, and formerly stood up at the head of the street.

Fig. 227

GIDEON BECK HOUSE, 152 COURT STREET, PORTSMOUTH

This little old house is shown on the Map of 1813, but was probably built much earlier. There is no definite data.

Fig. 228

SISE-LAIGHTON HOUSE (BEFORE 1813) 69 RICHARDS AVE., PORTSMOUTH

Shown on the Map of 1813. Built probably not much before, because the street was not opened until about 1800.

Fig. 229

WILLIAM HAVEN HOUSE, 240 MIDDLE STREET, PORTSMOUTH

Built soon after 1800 by William Haven, cashier of the New Hampshire Bank.

Fig. 230

ABRAHAM SHAW HOUSE, STATE STREET
AND A PRIVATEERSMAN'S PORTRAIT

Abraham Shaw, a wealthy merchant, owned this corner property as early as 1801, and it is said that he built this house during the war of 1812, with privateer money. He owned a number of armed ships, and his brother, Capt. Thomas Shaw, was a noted privateersman. The Shaw brothers were the owners of Shaw's Wharf, near Puddle Dock. In the lower hall is a fine oil painting of the first owner, Abraham Shaw, (Fig. 231).

Fig. 231

Fig. 232

ORACLE HOUSE (PROBABLY SOON AFTER 1709) HAYMARKET SQUARE, 37 COURT STREET, PORTSMOUTH

This little house formerly stood on the Glebe Land, directly back of the North Church. About 1800 it was moved to Haymarket Square. It has been called the Oracle House, because the Oracle of the Day was published here by Charles Peirce in 1793. It formerly stood on Lot No. 1 of the Glebe, which was leased by Richard Wibird, in 1709, and it is possible that he erected this house soon after. It has been preserved and moved to watertront in 1937

Fig. 233

DURHAM FLAGGING STONES, HAYMARKET SQUARE, PORTSMOUTH

The first street paving was in "Paved Street", now Market Street, in 1767.

The only reference we have of this old time sidewalk is made in Rev. Timothy Alden's Century Sermon, 1801, "We have but one paved street. One side of most of our streets has been paved with very nice flat stones from Durham, in such a manner that two or three persons can walk abreast. It is a European style of sidewalk and so rarely used in this country that it was formerly said the ladies of Portsmouth had a peculiar gait acquired by tripping over such stones as these."

Fig. 234

EDWARD PARRY HOUSE (REVOLUTIONARY DATE) 129 PARROTT AVE., PORTSMOUTH

This house formerly stood in Haven Park. Some think it was erected by Edward Parry, the unfortunate gentleman to whom 27 chests of tea were consigned in 1774. The Sons of Liberty mobbed his house and made him reship the tea to Halifax. He was suspected by the Sons of Liberty and so often troubled by them that he built a fort in his backyard, the remains of which may still be seen in the lower part of Haven Park. So it seems probable that the house was built just before the Revolution.

Fig. 235

NATHANIEL HAVEN HOUSE (1799) 44 HIGH STREET, PORTSMOUTH

Dr. Nathaniel Haven, son of Rev. Samuel Haven, built this house. The wrought iron Lantern Arch is graceful and recalls such lanterns still remaining in the streets of Mayfair.

Fig. 236

CAPTAIN THOMAS THOMPSON HOUSE (1784) 179 PLEASANT STREET, PORTSMOUTH

Built by Capt. Thomas Thompson, one of the first naval officers commissioned by the Continental Congress. Capt. Thompson commanded the Frigate Raleigh, built here in 1776.

This house is now the residence of Miss Susan Wentworth and contains the full length portraits of the Royal Governors of that name. The Greek porch is an apparent later alteration.

Fig. 237

HARRIS-HEFFENGER HOUSE, 43 AND 53 AUSTIN STREET, PORTSMOUTH

This double house was built before 1813. One of the windows bears the inscription scratched in the glass, "John Peirce, 1829."

Fig. 238

JEREMIAH MASON HOUSE (1808)

This house was built by Mason, of whom Daniel Webster said, "As a Jurist no man in the nation equalled Mason, and but one approached him." He meant Chief Justice Marshall. This great house was well in scale with its builder who was six and a half feet high.

Fig. 239

Fig. 240

159 MIDDLE STREET, PORTSMOUTH

Shown on the map of 1813. Evidently, the Greek porches and granite steps have been added later.

Fig. 241

CAPTAIN CHARLES BLUNT HOUSE, 383 PLEASANT STREET, PORTSMOUTH

No date, but built by Capt. Charles Blunt. Later, (in the 40's and 50's) it was lived in by Capt. March, a great builder of Clipper ships. From his yard came the "Franklin Peirce"—the "Frank Jones"—and the "Granite State."

Fig. 242

A Little Arbor in a Court Street Garden

Fig. 243

A Typical Portsmouth Tidal Mill-pond

Showing many early houses still standing in a group, with the Wentworth Gardner House in the centre.

Fig. 244

Garrison House of Robert Cutt (Circa 1660) Kittery, Maine
(later known as the Whipple House)

This land, on the back river known as "Crooked Lane", was deeded to Robert Cutt by the Town in 1651. According to Stackpole, he seems to have built soon after. The present house is much altered.

Fig. 245

RICHARD SHORTRIDGE HOUSE, DEER STREET, PORTSMOUTH

This house was built by Daniel Hart, previous to the Revolution. The exact date is not known. During the Revolution Mrs. Richard Shortridge kept a lodging-house here, and many officers from the French Fleet lodged at Mrs. Shortridge's house.

In 1850 the house was occupied by Peter Jenness and is often called the Peter Jenness House. It was evidently altered architecturally at that time. It is now a Home For Aged Women. The anecdote which follows is quoted verbatim from Brewster.

"Gov. Benning Wentworth was left a widower and childless.

In his loneliness he saw a young lady to whom he took a fancy. He proposed marriage—but Molly Pitman had given her heart to another, who, although of humble life, she esteemed more essential to her happiness than the honor and riches of the Governor,—and so she married Richard Shortridge, a mechanic, in preference. The Governor, however, did not forget the indignity of her refusal, and yet hoped by adopting David's unwise example, to conquer. An English frigate was in the harbor, and not long after the marriage a press gang was sent to the house of Shortridge, which forcibly took him on board, and from the endearments of home. For seven long years did his faithful wife mourn his absence. He was removed from ship to ship, until one day he related to the chief officer the circumstances under which he was impressed. 'Run off, and we won't pursue you,' was the reply; and he soon availed himself of the privilege. His return brought happiness to his faithful partner, whose virtue was not to be invaded by the most tempting allurements of wealth."

Fig. 246

LONG-LADD HOUSE (1812) 3 RICHARDS AVE., PORTSMOUTH

Built when the other three story brick houses were being built about town.

Fig. 247

TREADWELL-JENNESS HOUSE (1818) PORTSMOUTH

On this site stood the house of Thomas Packer, the hated Sheriff of the Province, who hanged Ruth Blay in 1768. The same night the indignant people hanged his effigy in front of his house, with this inscription:

"Am I to lose my dinner this woman for to hang?
Come draw away the cart, my boys don't stop to say Amen."

Fig. 248

ROGERS-HOYT HOUSE, 172 NORTHWEST STREET, PORTSMOUTH

The exact date of this house is not known. In the 1830's it was owned by George Rogers, a brick manufacturer, who carried on his business just east of the house.

Fig. 249

GRIFFIN HOUSE (BEFORE 1813) 552 STATE STREET, PORTSMOUTH

In the old days, this was the home of Capt. Matthew Vennard, a shipmaster. It is on the map of 1813.

Fig. 250

ENTRANCE TO ABRAHAM WENDELL HOUSE, PLEASANT STREET, PORTSMOUTH

A gracefully pompous doorway of 1815-20. Quite a London Georgian type.

Fig. 251

Abraham Wendell House (Circa 1813) 283 Pleasant Street, Portsmouth

Not shown on the map of 1813, but believed to have been built very soon thereafter. It was built by Abraham Wendell, son of Hon. John Wendell and brother of Jacob.

Fig. 252

Benedict House (Circa 1813) 30 Middle Street, Portsmouth

It is believed that this house was built by Captain George Libbey, shortly before 1813.

Fig. 253

"1705" House, 33 Deer Street, Portsmouth

This little house was built in 1705, as the date on the chimney shows, by John Newmarch, son of Rev. John Newmarch of Kittery, who also built the house next east, called the Deer Tavern, from which the street takes its name. His wife was a sister of Sir William Pepperrell.

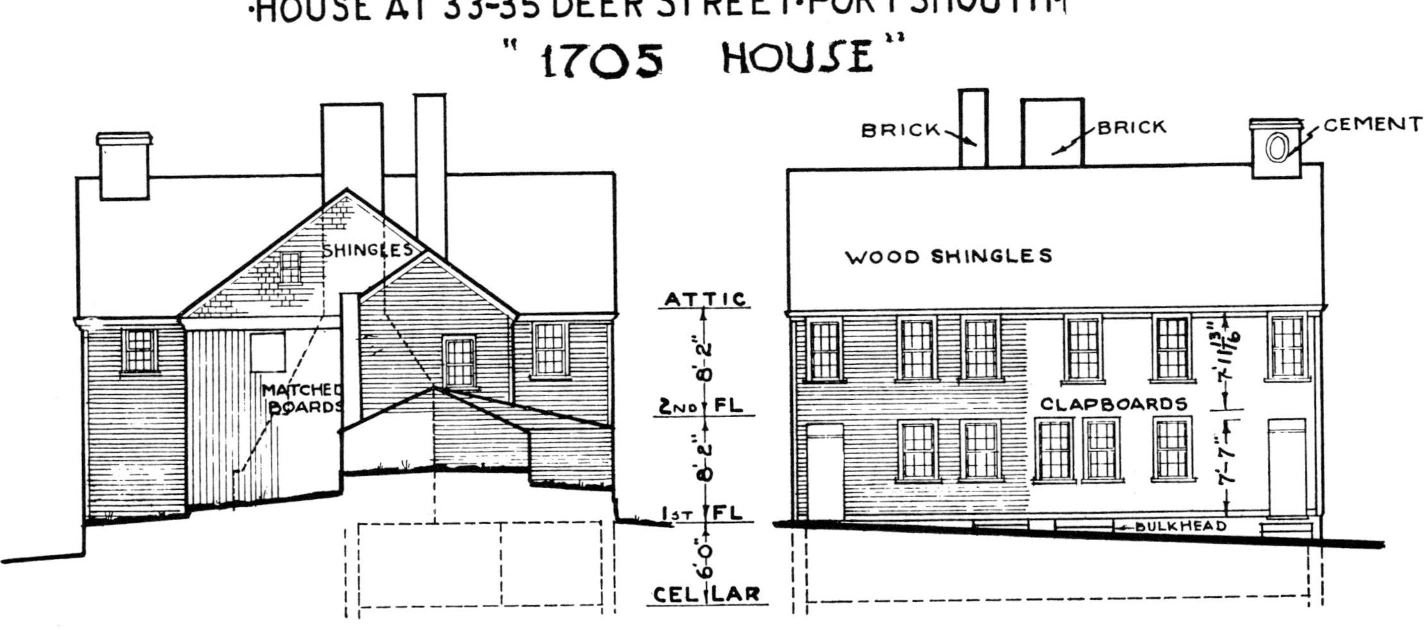

Historic American Buildings Survey—Library of Congress

Fig. 254

·HOUSE AT 33-35 DEER STREET·PORTSMOUTH·
BUILT 1705
"1705 HOUSE"
THESE EXTERIOR WALLS ARE OUT OF TRUE
OVENS
BAKER-SHOP
OLD STAIR ON CHIMNEY
K 14
BR 13
BR 12
LR 11
P 15
H 16
H 17
B.R.-28
LR 27
K-26
S.H 29
B.R. 23
L.R. 22
K-21
B.R. 24
H 25
ROOM IDENTIFICATION
H=HALL
C= CLOSET
P=PANTRY
K= KITCHEN
LR-LIVING-ROOM
BR=BED-ROOM
SH= OLD STAIR-HALL
SECOND FLOOR PLAN
FIRST FLOOR PLAN

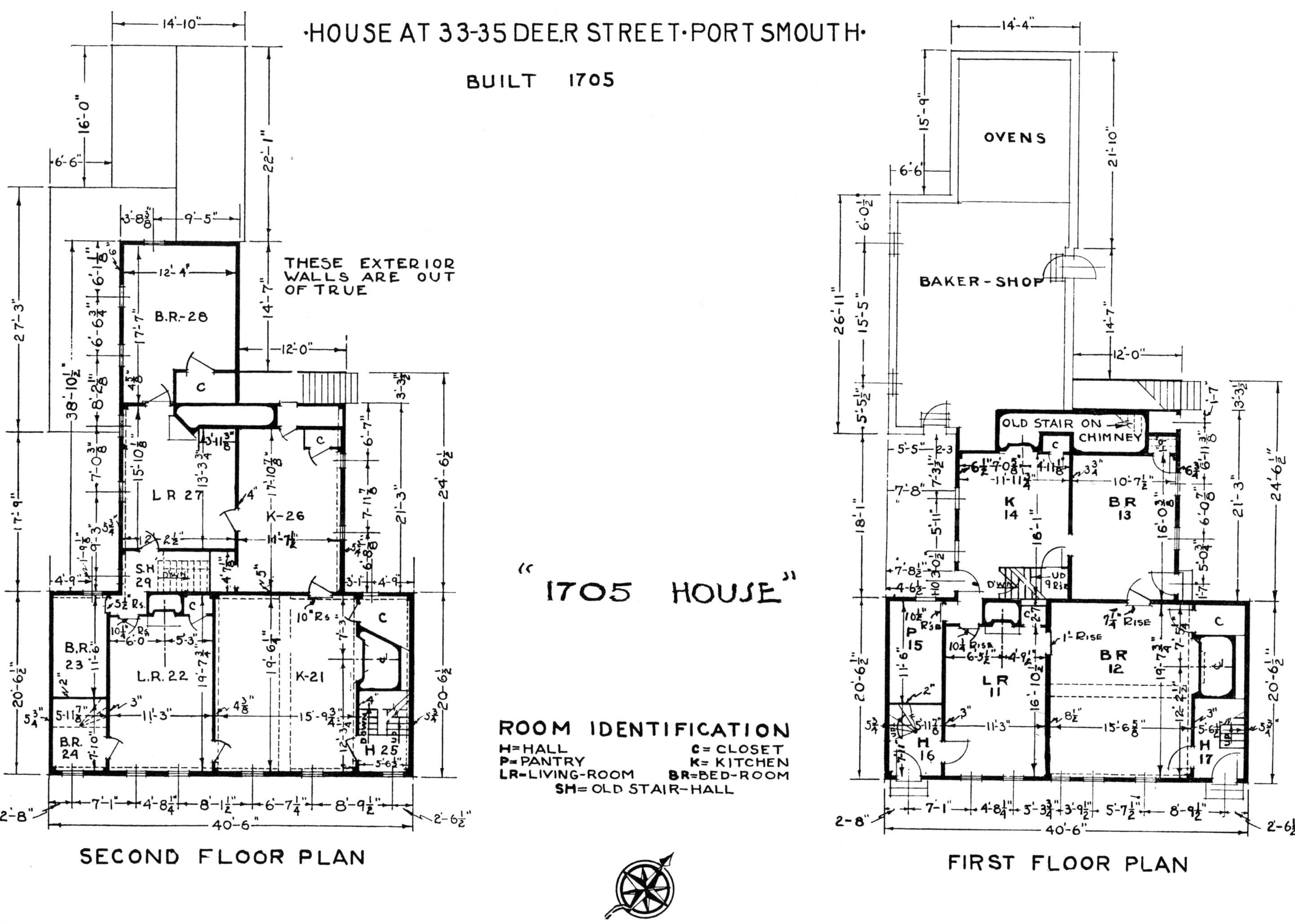

Fig. 255

DOOR TRIM
BOLECTION MOULD
OLD DOOR K26
3/4" THICK
1 1/8" STRIP TOP-MORTISED & TENONED
BALUSTER H-17
SQUARE
TURNED
PLAN
OLD CHIMNEY CAP
1705
CEMENT
POST-CAP
HAND-RAIL
STRING
FULL SIZE DETAILS
WHITE PINE
PLAN
BRICK
WOOD
PLASTER
FIREPLACE LR-27
INCHES
FEET
METRIC
RICHARD KOEHLER DEL.
CONTRIBUTED BY NHERA AND DEPARTMENT OF ARCHITECTURE UNIVERSITY OF NEW HAMPSHIRE
U.S. DEPARTMENT OF THE INTERIOR
OFFICE OF NATIONAL PARKS, BUILDINGS, AND RESERVATIONS
BRANCH OF PLANS AND DESIGN
·HOUSE AT 33-35 DEER STREET·PORTSMOUTH·ROCKINGHAM CO·NH·
NAME OF STRUCTURE
BUILT 1705
SURVEY NO.
N·H·10
HISTORIC AMERICAN BUILDINGS SURVEY
SHEET 6 OF 8 SHEETS
INDEX NO.

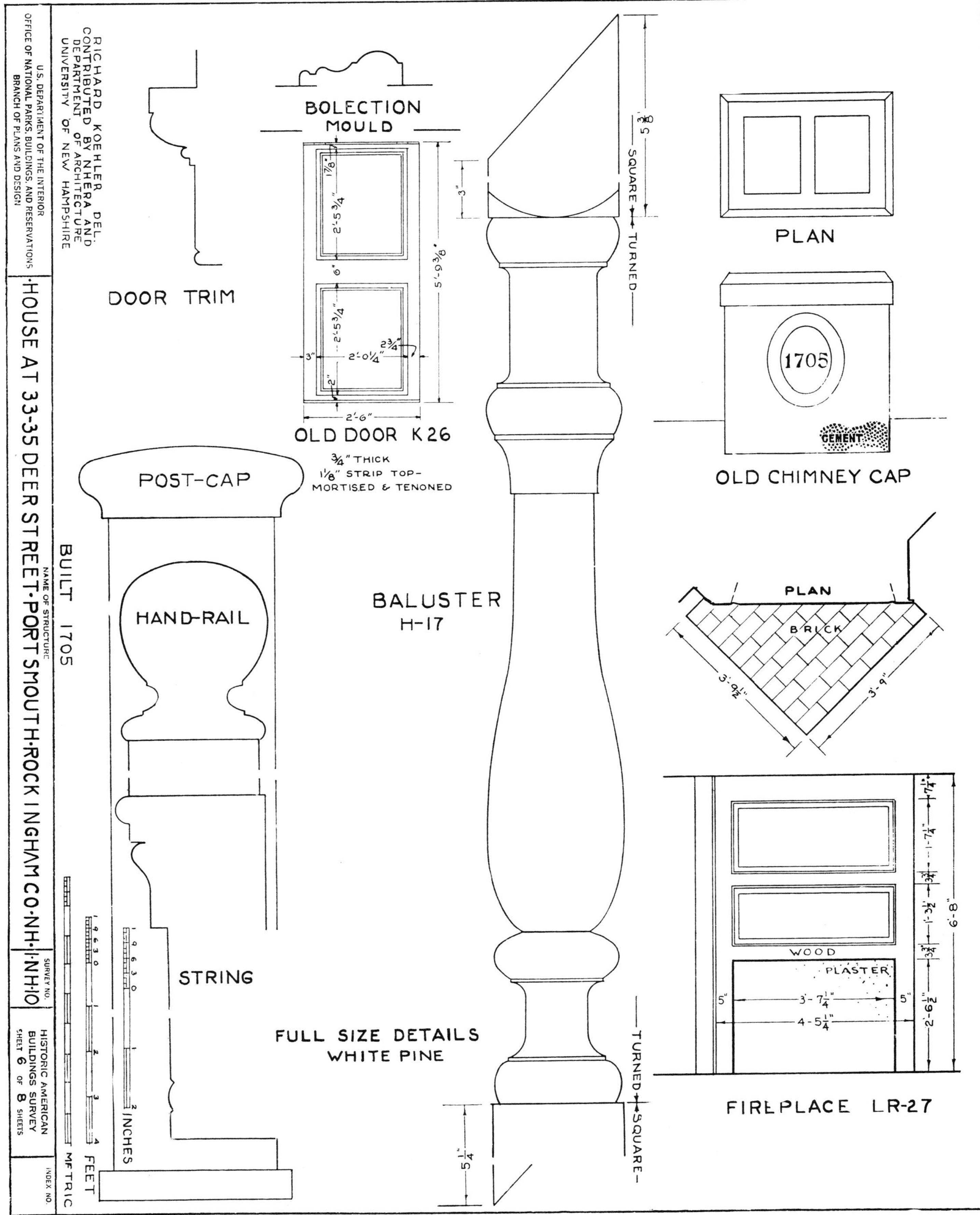

Fig. 256

Fig. 257

THE ATHENAEUM, MARKET SQUARE, PORTSMOUTH

This formal graceful building standing on the Parade (now usually called Market Square) was built in 1803 by John Peirce for the use of the New Hampshire Fire and Marine Insurance Co. which was failed by the War of 1812. The building was purchased in 1817 by the Proprietors of the Portsmouth Athenaeum. The cornice surmounted by a delicate balustrade formerly came down in a sweep or curve to meet the line of the cornice of the lower buildings on each side. This was a beautiful and graceful design, very original and worthy of the best architectural talent. Only one piece of curved cornice and no cornice balustrade remains.

Fig. 258

St. John's Church (1807) Chapel Street, Portsmouth

Built on the site of old Queen's Chapel. The church was destroyed by fire in 1806, and rebuilt the following year. The bell was brought from Louisburg in 1745 by William Pepperrell, and recast after the fire, by Paul Revere. The beautiful communion silver was given by Queen Caroline in 1732.

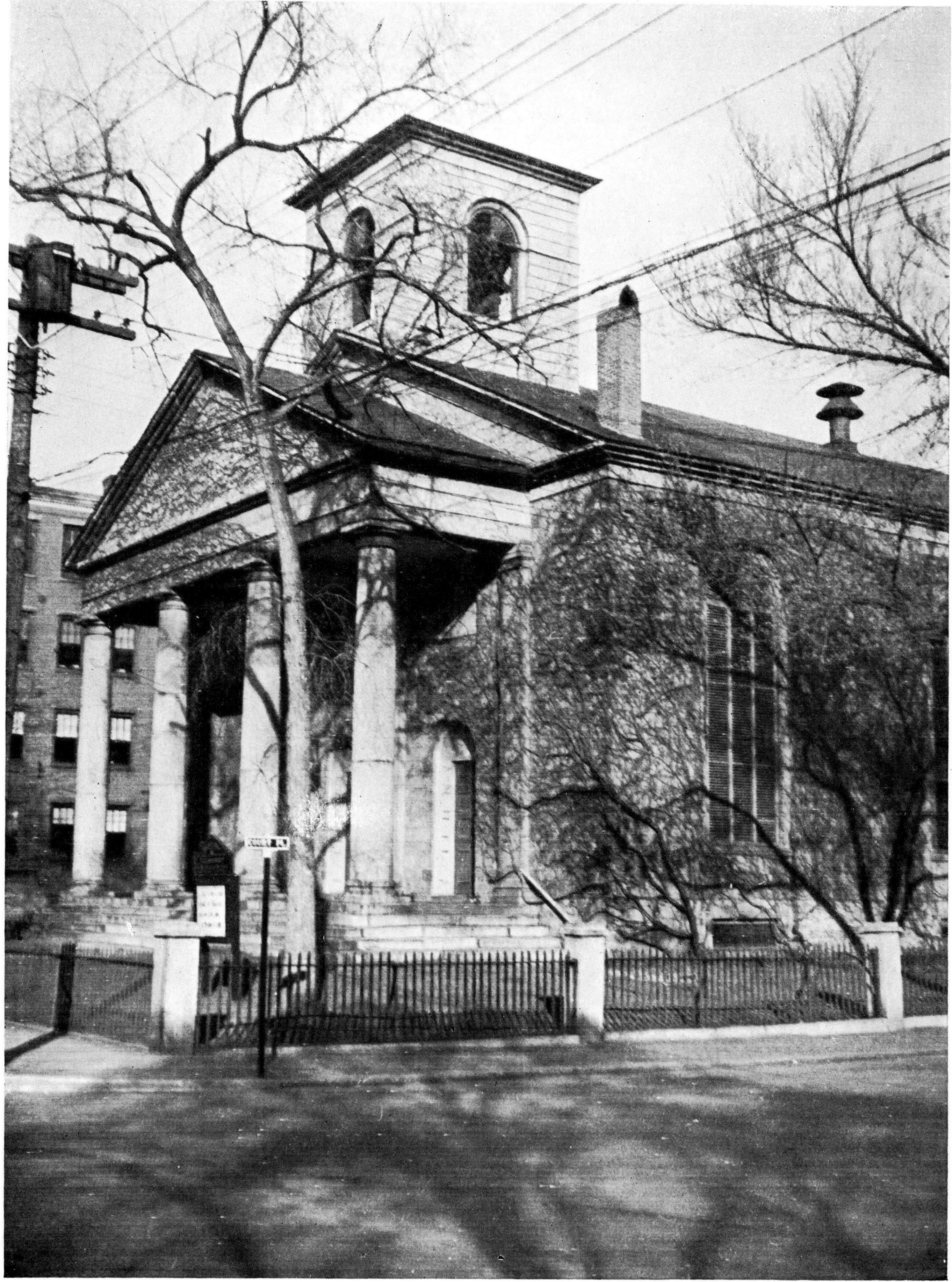

Fig. 259

South (Unitarian) Church, State Street, Portsmouth

Built in 1824 after the Great Fire, which began in Woodwards barn then standing on the exact spot now occupied by this church.

Fig. 260

SOUTH WARD ROOM, MEETING HOUSE HILL, PORTSMOUTH

In 1865 this building was erected on the site of the Old South Meeting House which had just been demolished. The old Meeting House had occupied this site since 1731, the land having been given to the town by John Pickering. The elevation has been called Meeting House Hill since the early days when the old church stood there.

Fig. 261

St. John's Chapel (1824) State Street, Portsmouth

This little building of much dignity and beauty, was built in 1824.

In 1732, the property was purchased by Jacob Sheafe of New Castle, who came here to make his home.

Fig. 262

Old Court House (1836) 175 Parrott Ave., Portsmouth

Stood on Court Street, where the Central Fire Station is now located. It was used for a Court House until 1891.

Fig. 263

A Dover Doorway

Dover, like Portsmouth, is on the Piscataqua river. It is nearly as ancient but today has a much smaller volume of early architecture.

Fig. 264

184 Deer Street, Portsmouth

This house stands with its end to the street, and this doorway is in the center of the side, entered through a garden. Occupied as early as 1839 by Frederick Mullens, a brass founder by trade. It has no particular history and no exact date of construction has been found.

Fig. 265

Henry Sherburne House (1725) Deer Street, Portsmouth—Front Entrance

Fig. 266

PORCH OF ROBERT FOLLETT HOUSE (1756) KITTERY POINT, MAINE

This porch is from an unidentified Portsmouth House. It was applied to the Follett house, itself much altered, about 1930.

Fig. 267

Shapley-Sise House (1799)
116 Middle Street, Portsmouth

Fig. 268

102 State Street, Portsmouth
After fire of 1813

Fig. 269

Nathaniel Haven House (1799)
44 High Street, Portsmouth

Fig. 270

Alfred Rundlet House
Middle Street, Portsmouth

Fig. 271

Jackson House—an Old Coach Entrance
School Street, Portsmouth

Fig. 272

Christopher Toppan House
163 Vaughan Street, Portsmouth

Fig. 273

Fernald House
434 Marcy Street, Portsmouth

Fig. 274

The Calico-Party House (before 1740)
93 Deer Street, Portsmouth

Fig. 275

Entrance Doorway and Fan Light
306 Marcy Street, Portsmouth

Fig. 276

George Dennett House, 314 Maplewood Ave.,
Christian Shore, Portsmouth

Fig. 277

Elisha Hill House (Circa 1800)
53 Court Street, Portsmouth

Fig. 278

Pierce House, 43 Manning Street
Off Meeting House Hill, Portsmouth

Fig. 279

LORD HOUSE
19 HOWARD STREET, PORTSMOUTH

Fig. 280

RICHARD TIBBETTS HOUSE
212 PLEASANT STREET, PORTSMOUTH

Fig. 281

177 STATE STREET, PORTSMOUTH
Built after the great fire of 1813

Fig. 282

175 STATE STREET, PORTSMOUTH
Built after the great fire of 1813

Fig. 283

40 Parker Street, Portsmouth
An interesting Greek Revival doorway

Fig. 284

Governor Ichabod Goodwin House (Circa 1811)
263 Islington Street, Portsmouth

Fig. 285

Edmonds House
86 Islington Street, Portsmouth

Fig. 286

Ichabod Rollins House (1790)
444 Pleasant Street, Portsmouth

Fig. 287

SHEAFE'S WAREHOUSE (1705) PORTSMOUTH

Sheafe's warehouse was built before 1705. Capt. Steward has a deed of it dated that year. It was once owned by Capt. Tobias Lear who built the "Ranger."

This very ancient warehouse still stands with its corbelled front hanging over the water at high tide. The sailing scows of that day called "Gondalows" and similar craft, were able to come in under the overhang at high water, and could be loaded or unloaded direct into the upper loft. Captain John Paul Jones here fitted out the "Ranger" and sailed to conquer His Majesty's ship "Drake" off the Isle of Man, he flying the flag made for him by the young women of Portsmouth. This was the first American flag to take a salute from the guns of European powers—when he took the "Drake" as a prize into Brest.

This ancient building is set on cob-work like a wharf.

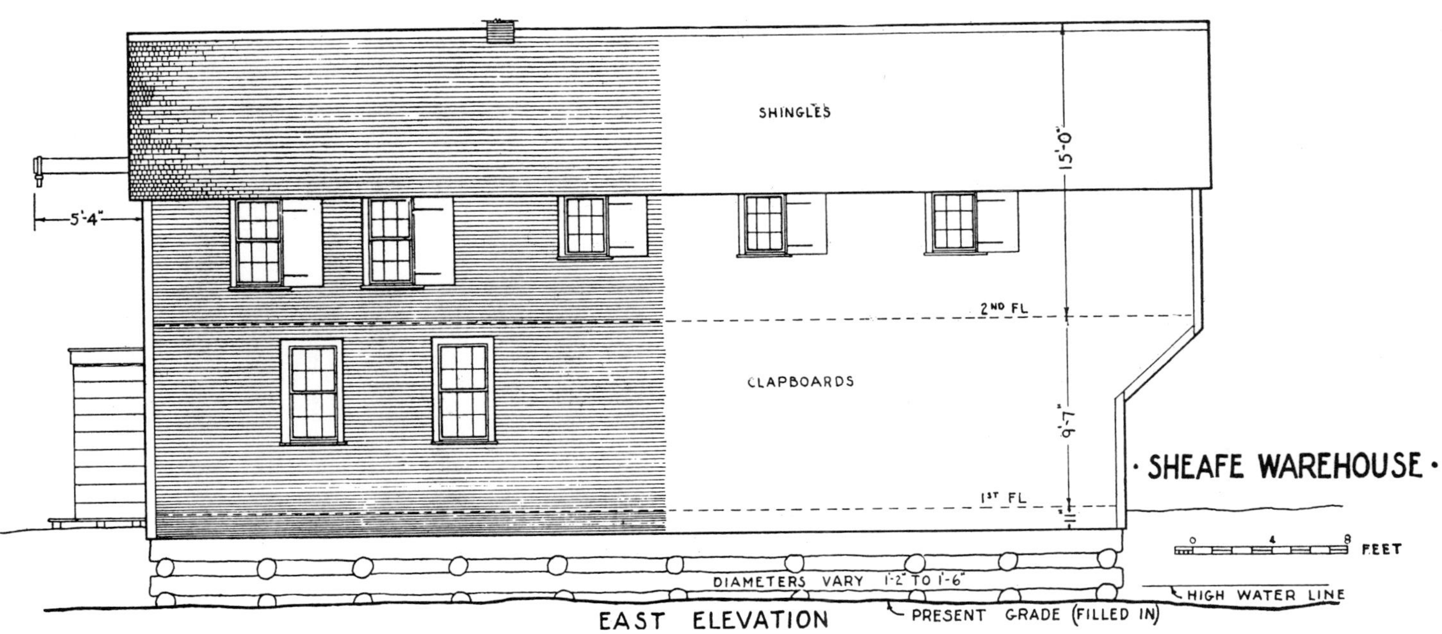

Fig. 288

Fig. 289

Block House, Fort McClary, Kittery Point, Maine

There has been a fort on this site since 1715 but there seems to be no exact date for this blockhouse. There are ports in the overhang from which to shoot or pour down water. The building to the left is a powder house, with double walls and a heavy brick vault. The space above the vault and under the roof is filled with field stones.

Fig. 290

Billings House (before 1794) Kittery Point

This shows at both ends the characteristic wings or "Beverly Ears" giving second story windows looking seaward.

Fig. 291

FRANCIS HOOKE HOUSE (BEFORE 1674) ON THE PISCATAQUA AT KITTERY POINT, MAINE

"Francis Hooke, a son of Humphrey Hooke, an Alderman of the City of Bristol, England, bought of Nicholas Shapleigh, 4. Aug. 1674 three acres of land whereon was a house or tenement formerly built possessed and enjoyed by Roger Russell."

The piazzas are a late addition.

Fig. 292

A TIDEWATER HOUSE AT KITTERY POINT, MAINE

Most early houses were built like this one on backwaters—safer and more convenient for the vessels of the day, for even their trading brigs were small enough to lie at their cob wharfs in these creeks, and to rest on the mud at low water.

One of the earlier owners was shanghai'd and away for two years, during which time he is said to have been sold out by the holder of his mortgage.

Fig. 293

TOMB OF COL. GEORGE BOYD (1787) OLD NORTH CEMETERY, PORTSMOUTH

Col. Boyd had this stone cut in England and brought it with him on his return to Portsmouth. Two days before the ship reached port he died.

TOMB STONE OF COL. GEORGE BOYD

2" DEEP SUNK PANEL FOR INSCRIPTION SLAB WHICH IS MISSING

3 · 8½ · 1-4 · 8½ · 3 · 3-3

3 · ¾ · 1-6½ · ¾ · 3-2 · 7⅛ · 1¼ · 4⅜ · 1¼ · 3 · 10

TOP VIEW

6-6

5 · 2-2 · 6 · 3-1

3-3

INSCRIPTION ON SLAB

GEORGE BOYD ESQUIRE FORMER MERCHANT OF THIS TOWN WHO AFTER MANY YEARS EMBARKED AT LONDON FOR HIS NATIVE TOWN IN AUGUST 1787 BUT TO THE GREAT GRIEF OF HIS WIFE CHILDREN AND FRIENDS HE DEPARTED THIS LIFE ON THE 6TH DAY OF OCTOBER 1787 AGE 54 TWO DAYS BEFORE MAKING PORT.

SOURCE
CEMETERY INSCRIPTIONS by ARTHUR H. LOCK

Fig. 294

Fig. 295

Courtesy of Honorable William E. Marvin

PORTSMOUTH PIECES, CIRCA 1816

Sofa and Sideboard in the 1815 home of Langley Boardman, (see plate 62), the wealthy cabinet maker. From 1800 to 1820, Portsmouth was one of our largest cities, and shipped fine furniture to the West Indies, etc. Stephen Decatur, Esq., in his writings on Langley Boardman, attributes these pieces to him.

Fig. 296

Courtesy of Honorable William E. Marvin

Fig. 297

Courtesy of Honorable William E. Marvin

PORTSMOUTH CHAIRS (CIRCA 1816)

The Chair with rosetted back is regarded as typical of the work of Langley Boardman.

Fig. 298

CARVED EAGLE OF COLONIAL CHARACTER

This is thought to be from the stern transom of a ship said to have been dismantled at Portsmouth. Bottom of tail and fasces are restorations. Wing spread about ten feet.

Fig. 299

Martin Frost House (1732) Eliot, Maine—but originally Kittery, Mass., before the separation of Maine.

This photograph shows an early original stencilled wall decoration executed in a lime and milk mixture, which long remained unsuspected under the wall paper in the hall. This is just as discovered and possibly put on shortly after the house was built in 1732. The Frost family obtained the land then, as a town grant, and still lives on it. The wall background is a fairly dark smoky blue, with the stencilled figures in black and red.

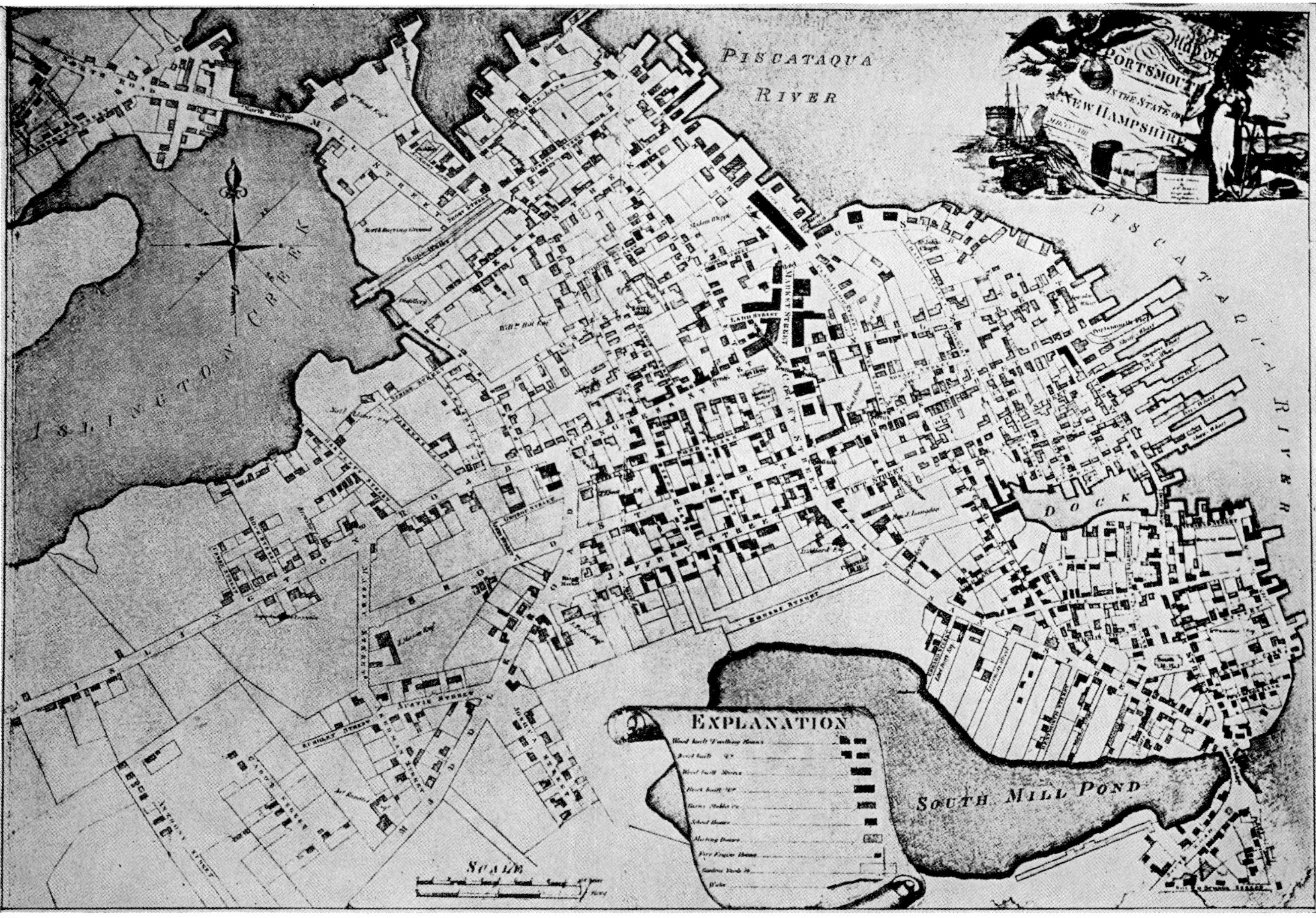

Fig. 300

THE 1813 MAP OF PORTSMOUTH, NEW HAMPSHIRE

This map was evidently completed in 1813 before the great fire which destroyed so large an area including many of the finer and older houses. There is also a map dated 1812, which hangs, framed, in a mutilated condition in the City Hall, but everything to the east of Water Street, where it crosses the Puddle Dock, is missing.

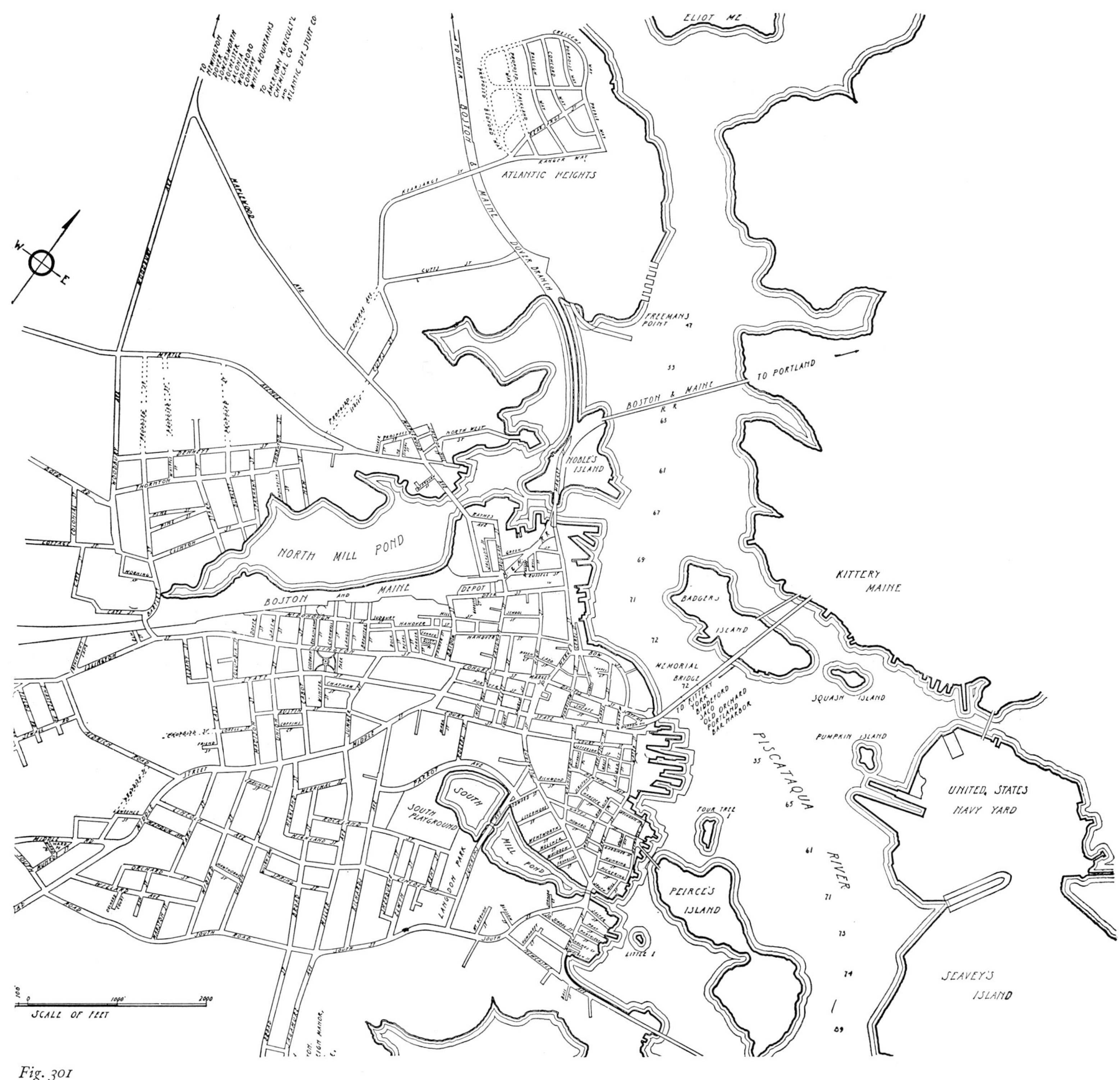

Fig. 301

PORTSMOUTH, NEW HAMPSHIRE, AS IT IS TODAY

INDEX OF PLATES